With Respect for Others: Activities for a Global Neighborhood

by Cynthia M. Manthey

Humanics Learning

Humanics Learning
P.O. Box 7400
Atlanta, GA 30357

Design and Illustrations by Susan Chamberlain

PRINTED IN THE UNITED STATES OF AMERICA

Library of Congress Cataloging-in-Publication Data

Manthey, Cynthia M., 1961-
    With respect for others: activities for a global neighborhood/by Cynthia M. Manthey
        p. cm.
    Includes bibliographical references and index.
        ISBN 0-89334-241-6 (pbk.). -- ISBN 0-89334-247-5 (1ib. bdg.)
        1. Multicultural education -- Activity programs -- United States.
    2. Early childhood education -- Activity programs -- United States.
    I. Title.
    LC1099.3.M25 1995
    370.19'6--dc20

                                                                    95-21242
                                                                        CIP

DEDICATION

To two people who look down upon no one - my friends Dawn and Art Shegonee.

Pillars of Importance
Look
   down
      upon
         others
            no
               longer.

It's
   time
      to
         view
            things
               eye to eye.

by Cynthia M. Manthey

ACKNOWLEDGMENTS

My heartfelt thanks to the following people for their support, encouragement and sincere interest in sharing information and thoughts which have shaped this book into what it is now:

Michael Oladejo Afolayan, Ph.D.; Professor Richard Flotez; Jesus Avilla; Maria Avilla; Teresa Lichte; Yvonne Thomas; Positive Images African American Art Gallery, Madison, WI; Professor Gilles Busquette; Kayla Chepyator; Tapologo Mandeni; Anita Sutter; Teresa Lichte; Lee Burkholder and the other wonderful people at Global Express, Madison, WI; and my husband, Dennis.

TABLE OF CONTENTS

INTRODUCTION

Welcome to *With Respect for Others: Activities for a Global Neighborhood.* This is a volume of primary theme units to be used by teachers at the Early Childhood level. Primary theme units are those which are the main focus of planned events. Weekly secondary units can consist of other themes such as a number, a letter, or a shape. The objectives within this series include fostering children's sense of respect for self, others, and the world.

This series of books is intended to be used as a starting point or supplement to curriculum development. Consider it a seed from which a whole garden of ideas can grow. In other words, feel free to expand upon, add to, or adapt these activities as your children desire. In keeping with a developmentally appropriate approach, we must all allow great flexibility for change within our planned activities.

Several multicultural units are presented within this volume along with units on sensory awareness and self-esteem. Your children and their families must also be included in your program to offer exploration of the cultural diversity right within each individual classroom. For children who come from multi-racial families, take plenty of time with parents to discuss what aspects of these cultures they would like to see in their child's environment. Certain people, for cultural, religious, or personal reasons wish to remain very private - which must also be respected. If your school or day care consists of an array of cultures, you have a wonderful opportunity to invite family members as resource persons to work with when developing your activity plans. Although many environments are uniracial, it is still possible to explore beautiful, individual differences.

On a daily basis, cruelty and injustice among your children must be dealt with immediately as it arises. Many times activities can be developed from these situations. Whether the cruelty stems from differences in age, appearance, gender, physical capability, family, race, culture, or countless other sources, it can be turned into a positive learning experience for children. Remember to type up a note for parents to explain these sensitive issues and inform them that they were handled. In this manner, you may assist parents in realizing their own hidden prejudices, their harmful effects, and how these opinions can inadvertently be passed on to children.

Remember to keep your environment multicultural on an ongoing basis. Inclusion of multicultural toys, dramatic play props, visual aids, books, stories, music, food, visitors, and trips will help your children to see that every person, family, home, and lifestyle is unique. How can our children's respect and appreciation for differences in others flourish if they are not allowed the opportunity to explore and experience differences with all of their senses?

It can be debated as to whether global awareness is appropriate for children at the Early Childhood level. Children are naturally and non-judgmentally curious about their world at this tender point in their lives. They are also very vulnerable to negative influences. Many problems within today's society exist because of the self-centeredness that is present within so many adults. We must help children to realize at a very early age that other people are important, even if they live on the other side of the earth, sleep when we are awake, and speak differently. It is this book's goal to have children of ages 3 and 4 recognize aspects of different countries and relate to those places or cultures with a sense of caring, knowledge and self-assurance...rather than with unnecessary fear.

Please include a globe within your learning environment as well as a world atlas made especially for children. (See Appendix for Multicultural Resources) Ask parents to supply you with information on places they will be traveling for business and/or vacation. If children have parents who are away on business trips or one who lives in another location, they can feel proud to be able to pull out an atlas and show their friends exactly where that parent is.

Sesame Street is an example of excellence in multicultural and global awareness presented in a respectful and interesting manner. Small children can connect with faraway places in many ways, including learning a few words from other languages and visualizing beautiful art, dance, or music from other cultures. Along with appreciating differences, children can learn the commonness we all share as human beings and as citizens of the same world.

We are now aware of the many different cultures within our own country which have been oppressed for hundreds of years. Now is the time to allow freedom of culture, including language, dress, religion, music, celebrations, and dietary preferences. Let's not shield our children from the splendor of other cultures. Public Native American Pow-Wows, African (along with many other cultures') dance demonstrations, and ethnic festivals are not only suitable for young children, but also are extremely beneficial. Showing the diversity of both traditional and contemporary aspects of cultures or countries is essential when teaching children global awareness and multicultural respect.

Neither this text nor any other single book should be your entire "multicultural curriculum." The intention of this book is to inspire teachers to incorporate multiculturalism into their lessons on an ongoing basis. It can be a starting point from which a sense of caring and respect for others can begin. As you use this book, please consult each unit's introductory page for ideas to incorporate throughout your entire curriculum. Hopefully, this book will encourage you to delve into other multicultural resources. The best resource, of course, is real people. Invite special guests and visitors into your classroom to become involved with you and your children. Remember: the children and families you work with must be included with your multicultural education. Most people are proud to share information about their cultures. Your sincere interest and respect can give them hope for retaining their cultural identity. Teaching children to respect cultural differences today will help build the foundation of peace for future generations.

UNIT ONE
Self-Empowerment & Self-Esteem

UNIT ONE: Self-Empowerment & Self-Esteem
Introduction

As you know, children in their early childhood years are very easily impressed by what they see and hear. What an ideal time to impress upon them that they are much too valuable to ever use drugs! At this tender age, we need not provide great detail about the types of drugs people abuse and their horrendous effects. We can, however, make a lasting impression upon children and present them with these facts:

• We are all VIPs! We are too good to let anything or anyone hurt our minds and bodies.

• We have the power to make our own good choices - even when our friends attempt to persuade us to make poor ones. (Peers and siblings - not strangers in trench coats - are eventually the biggest and most effective pushers of illegal drugs.)

• Drugs hurt people and are illegal.

• Medicines are helpful drugs. Small children can become very confused when they hear that drugs are bad, and subsequently hear an adult say they are going to the pharmacy to get some drugs.

• Medicine should only be given by a trusted adult. If a child finds any substance that looks like a food or beverage, he or she should immediately get an adult to help them.

• Police officers are community helpers who want to keep people safe. Television programs often confuse children by having the star of the movie or program fleeing from the "cops." If you've ever heard children during their dramatic play make statements such as, "Let's get out of here! The cops are going to get us!" explain to them the positive and necessary role that police officers hold in our society.

• If someone we don't know (a stranger) coaxes us to eat or drink something or come along with them, we should simply say, "No!" and run away.

So many of children's and adult's abuse against one another stems from bad feelings about themselves. The following is one experience which exemplifies this: A nine-year-old, vivacious, extremely bright girl with Cerebral Palsy, able to speak very few words, was verbally attacked by a newcomer to her school. The "attacker," who happened to be a boy, yelled things such as, "You can't talk! What's wrong with you? At least I can talk!" repeatedly until the girl was crying inconsolably. As it turns out, the boy was a special needs child himself who had been receiving speech therapy since kindergarten. His attempt to build up his own pride was accomplished by slashing someone else's. It is important for children to know that abuse stems from insecurity, and that treating others with respect is a sign of strength and self-esteem. Use the activities in this unit which help build a child's sense of self, trust, self-esteem, competence, powerfulness, and self-control.

UNIT ONE: Self-Empowerment & Self-Esteem (Letter to Parents)

Date:

Dear Parents:

This week our primary topic will be "Self-Empowerment & Self-Esteem." We will bring up the topic of drugs to find out what the children know and to answer their questions. The experiences of children during their early childhood years influence them greatly throughout their adolescent and adult lives. To overload these youngsters with facts about the composition, classification, or effects of drugs could cause them undue stress. However, by reaffirming their self-worth and self-power to make wise choices we can help them greatly at this age.

Here are some of the basic concepts we will incorporate during our activities relating to our topic:

• We are all too important and too smart to allow anyone or anything to harm us.

• We have the power to say, "No!" to friends who want us to make bad choices - even if it means losing their friendship. After all, peers and older siblings are the biggest pushers of alcohol and drugs to other children. "Misery loves company."

• Drugs can hurt our minds and bodies.

• Drugs are illegal.

• Medicines are helpful drugs. Many children are confused when they hear a loved one say they "need to go to the drug store" or they are "buying drugs" when in fact the adult is referring to medication.

• Medication should only be given by a trusted adult. If a child finds an edible-looking substance, it should be left alone and a parent or caregiver should be consulted.

• Police officers want to help keep people safe. They are NOT bad guys. Due to misleading television programs, many children can be heard during play making statements such as, "Hurry up before the cops get us!"

• If someone we don't know offers us something such as a toy, candy, etc., yell "No!" and run away.

Please let your child know how important it is to be able to talk together about any questions or problems that may come up. Ask your child questions such as, "Is medicine a good drug?" "What do bad drugs do to people?" "What would you do if you found something that looked like candy?"

Thank you for boosting your child's self-esteem by showing that what he or she is learning about is important to you.

Sincerely,

WITH RESPECT

ACTIVITY 1: "No!"

Objectives: Teach children that they can say "No," whole language and reading skills.

Materials:
- small rectangles cut from construction paper
- a marker
- tape or putty adhesive

Preparation: Print the word, "no" on many construction paper rectangles. Post the words on the walls and hide them in easy-to-find locations.

Procedure: Have the children search for the NO papers, allowing them to keep the ones they find. As the children find the words, have them say, "No" loudly. Tell the children that these NO papers are to help them remember that it's okay to tell people, including our friends, "No."

After playing the game, provide plenty of blank paper rectangles along with other paper and markers for them to write their own NO papers if they'd like.

Tips: Save a few reserved NO papers to give to children who don't manage to locate any.

Additional Activity: Print several short words on paper rectangles (including several rectangles with the word "No.") Post all of the rectangle words. Allow the children to sort the rectangles by placing the ones which say, "No" into a container marked, "No."

NO patterns for children to decorate.

ACTIVITY 2: I Can Say, "No!" to My Friends

Objectives: Self-Empowerment skills, writing and drawing skills, and creative expression.

Materials:
- large construction paper sheets
- markers or crayons
- a "No" paper rectangle from the preceding activity for each child
- *optional:* scissors, yarn, paper scraps, and glue

Preparation: Have the children draw pictures of their friends, including siblings. Ask who each friend is and label each drawing if the child agrees to allow you to write on his or her paper. The children may cut yarn hair, paper clothes, or other details and glue them on if desired.

Procedure: Give each child a "No" rectangle. Ask them to print this word on their friend drawings to help them remember that they can tell anyone, "No" if they are asked to do something wrong, dangerous, or against the rules. You may wish to write the word "No" in dots for some children and ask them to connect the dots. For children who are unable to print letters, you may wish to hold their hand and help them write while saying the letters as you write them. If they would rather not write the word, "No" or don't want your assistance – that's fine. For less-abled children, you may supply them with glue and paper rectangles which say, "No" and allow them to glue them onto their paper.

Ask the Children: Even though we care about our friends, sometimes friends can tell us to do things that are wrong or dangerous. What should we tell our friends then? What if they won't be our friend anymore if we don't do what they want us to do? Will we ever get new friends?

ACTIVITY 3: N-O Spells NO! (Poem)

Objectives: Personal safety, self-empowerment, and communication skills.

Procedure: The teacher can say the verses alone, and the children can say the refrain along with the teacher, getting slightly louder with each "No!" Clapping along with this rhythmic poem makes it even more fun.

Refrain:
>   N-O spells NO! N-O spells NO!
>   No, no, no, no, - No, No, NO!
>
>   My friend can't tell me to cross the street.
>   Mom says to hold her hand.
>   My friend can't make me cross the street
>   'cause I - say - "No!" *(To refrain)*
>
>   Don't tell me to play with matches.
>   I know that those are hot!
>   My friend can't make me play with matches
>   'cause I - say - "No!" *(To refrain)*
>
>   I can stay safe. I can stay smart.
>   I know what to say that's in my heart.
>   I tell my friends, "I know what's right."
>   'cause I - say - "No!" *(To refrain)*

ACTIVITY 4: Find and Seek Help - Accidental Poisoning Prevention

Objectives: Safety, building self-esteem.

Materials: *One of the following items for each child:*
- a clear plastic bottle with a non-toxic colored liquid in it
- an empty medicine or vitamin container with a few small rocks in it
- pieces of candy (both wrapped and unwrapped including some which look like pills)
- a partially-filled glass of water
- a reward for each child (such as a sticker or a homemade award *see pattern illustration)
- something special that each child **may** eat

Preparation: Place each of the objects listed above in easy-to-locate spots. Instruct the children that when they spot something they think is a "danger" to taste, they should call out, "Help!" If a grownup does not respond, they should not touch the substance, but find an adult and show them the "dangerous" item. Photocopy the reward pattern for each child and write their names on them. Hand these out at the end of the activity.

Procedure: One by one, bring each child near the area that one of the items from above is hiding.

You can pretend to be working near the area where the child has located the "dangerous" item. Sometimes you should respond to the "Help" calls and sometimes you should ignore them to see that the children will actually come and ask for your help. After you see what the child is calling you for, hold up the "dangerous" item for the other children to see, place it out of reach, and give the help-seeking child a reward for doing a great job of staying safe.

After this role-play has been done with each child, have them wash their hands and give them something that **is** okay for them to eat. This reassures the children that there are caring, trustworthy adults who will give them snacks which are harmless.

Tips: This activity should not be done with any children prone to putting things in their mouths, since the candies being used could be choking hazards. Also, you may want to enlist the help of several other adults in this activity to make it easier for you.

WITH RESPECT

CONGRATULATIONS!

_____
NAME

You have successfully identified D-A-N-G-E-R!

SIGNED BY: _____

DATE: _____

ACTIVITY 5: Police Officers are for Helping People

Objectives: Promoting positive attitudes towards police officers, and the recognition of women in community service positions.

Preparation: Invite a local police officer to visit your school while the topic of "Drugs" is being taught. After calling to make an appointment for a visit, send the officer a copy of the letter on this page. Date the letter, fill in the officer's name, date, and time of the scheduled visit, and sign the letter. See the following extended activity: Police Badges.

Dear Officer:

Thank you for agreeing to visit us on _____ at _____.
$\qquad\qquad\qquad\qquad\qquad\qquad\qquad$ *Date* $\qquad\quad$ *Time*

Our preschool topic for that week will be "Self-Empowerment & Self-Esteem." The idea which we wish to impress upon the children is that they have the power to make wise choices, even when friends or siblings may coax them to break safety rules and do something that may hurt them.

Another one of our goals this week is for the children to understand that police officers are women and men who work to help keep people safe. Children these days can often be heard making statements such as, "Hurry up - the cops are coming!" while playing. Television and movies undoubtedly can have a negative influence upon children's opinions about police officers.

Due to the ages of the children, attention spans are quite short when they must sit still and listen. We invite you to read or tell a short story to the children. If you have any specific safety issues that are of particular interest, feel free to share your thoughts with the children.

We would like to request that you do not wear a gun. When small children see guns it can often be frightening or distracting, and sidetrack your entire purpose for this friendly visit. If you have any items having to do with personal safety such as stickers, pencils or coloring books that you wish to share with the children, please feel free to do so. There are _____ children in our class.

If you have any further questions before you come, please call. We hope your visit will spark many positive attitudes and relationships between law enforcement officials and today's children – tomorrow's adults.

Sincerely,

WITH RESPECT

ACTIVITY 6: Police Badges

Objectives: Dramatic play, safety skills.

Materials:
- the badge patterns
- foil scraps

For the Teacher:
- masking tape
- black permanent marker

Preparation: Photocopy the page of badges onto a heavy piece of paper. Cut each badge apart. Older children can cut out their own badges. Allow younger children to cut up other paper scraps in order for them to feel included. Blunt tip Fiskars brand scissors are the type we've seen the greatest success with since they cut through so many materials (i.e. yarn, felt, posterboard) and will cut easily at many different angles.

Procedure: Give each child a badge, and have them wrap the badge with foil. Help each child write his or her name on the badge with a permanent marker. Place a loop of masking tape on the back of each one so the children can wear them for dramatic play. One dramatic play idea would be to "swear in" the children as honorary safety officers, asking each child a safety question and then giving them their badges.

Tip: Please help teach your children to say, "Police Officer" rather than "PoliceMAN" since there are many women police officers. These badges can be made by the teacher beforehand or the children may wish to take part in making them.

ACTIVITY 7: ME Booklets

Objectives: Promote child's sense of self, artistic skills.

Materials:
- paper
- crayons
- glue
- scraps of paper or material
- yarn

Preparation: In the course of a week, give the children a variety of subjects to draw. The subjects might include self-portraits, family portraits, pets, the child's home, handprints, footprints, animals, favorite toys, etc.

Procedure: Keep the children's drawings and staple them together or tie them with yarn at the end of the week. Colored construction paper may be decorated and used as a cover to make the booklet appear more important. Send the booklets home with the children or ask to display them on a table in your library.

ACTIVITY 8: Trusting Your Feelings

Objectives: Developing child's sense of self-expression, communication skills. This will help children to recognize and accept their own feelings. This activity lays the groundwork for developing empathy.

Materials:
  • books on emotions or feelings (see Appendix for suggestions)

Preparation: Have the children sit in a carpeted area or arrange the desks in a circle.

Procedure: Read these books and talk about the feelings expressed. Ask the children if they have ever felt those emotions, letting them know that what they have felt is perfectly natural and okay. Let the children know that you are there for them even if they are hurt or angry or have bad feelings. By learning to trust and understand their own feelings, children can learn to resolve conflict within and with others at an early age.

ACTIVITY 9: "I Like Myself" Song and Poem

Objectives: Self-Esteem, rhythm, and gross-motor skills.

Movements:

clap 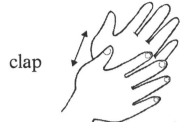   point to yourself

point to your friends

hug yourself

hands out to the sides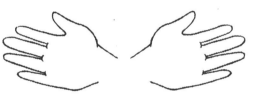

touch the floor and gradually move hands up towards the ceiling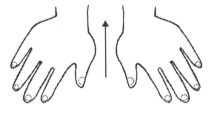

jump up, keeping hands up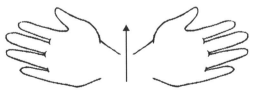

Refrain: I LIKE MYSELF!

I LIKE myself!   I LIKE myself!

I Like ME!

Verse: I'm GOOD! I'm SPECIAL!

I'm growing BIG! *(to refrain)*

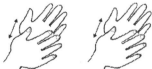

I LOVE myself!   I LOVE myself!

I love ME! *(to verse)*

I love YOU!   I love YOU!

I love YOU!
(Everyone gives a group hug.)

Tips: Allow everyone plenty of room for this exercise. Try to schedule this for a time when the children need to release some energy.

UNIT TWO
African Cultural Aspects

AFRICA

UNIT TWO: African Cultural Aspects
Introduction

When one thinks of Africa, images of a dark continent with massive jungles, widespread starvation, primitive tribes, and wild animals may come to mind. The words "jungle," "tribes," and "primitive" are not accepted as respectful when describing aspects of Africa. The word "forests" can replace the word "jungles." The wild animals are now mostly found in game reserves, game parks, and zoos. It is true that there is starvation in some parts of Africa; however, many of the world's wealthiest people live there, as well. The people of Africa are far from primitive. There are people there who live in enormously developed cities, as well as people who live in small villages. Also, Africa is not a country, it is a continent with approximately 55 distinct countries with thousands of different languages spoken throughout them.

Attempting to teach very young children aspects of every African country would be impossible. It is important for children to understand, however, that there are people who live in far-away places and that all of their family members of long-ago immigrated to America, or were brought here against their will. The exception to this being Native American people, who were in America first. Generating children's curiosity and enthusiasm for other places and peoples can encourage respect, concern, and care for them.

The activities in this unit are to promote awareness of African culture and traditions. By showing the children how varied and diverse the lives of African peoples are, the children will learn to identify with and not categorize the inhabitants of this continent. We can help children to feel that they are not only important and useful citizens of their families or schools, but also citizens of their communities, their countries, and the earth.

Contact a local travel agency for posters and brochures with colorful photos of Africa. National Geographic Magazine is an excellent source for finding photos of specific foreign cultures. Use this magazine with caution in order to prevent showing children only exotic aspects of cultures. It is important to allow the children to visualize diversity, including similarities and differences within city and country lifestyles on the continent of Africa.

UNIT TWO: African Cultural Aspects (Letter to Parents)

Date:

Dear Parents:

This week our primary focus will be on cultural aspects of some of the countries of Africa. One could easily spend a lifetime studying Africa. However, taking into consideration the age levels of the children, we will not go into great depth. We will be exploring the fact that Africa is truly a continent rich in diversity.

Many of the present misconceptions of Africa include ideas such as the following: Africa is all "jungle" with many wild animals; Africans are all starving; people who live there are "primitive tribespeople"; Africa is a country.

In reality, Africa is a huge continent with approximately 55 distinct countries and thousands of spoken languages. People living in Africa are far from primitive. There are people who live in large cities, and people who live in remote villages. Although starvation is a problem in some parts of Africa, many of the world's wealthiest people live there. We will touch lightly upon the topic of hunger during this unit in order to promote compassion, learn gratitude, and reduce wastefulness. The words, "jungle" and "tribes" are no longer considered respectful when describing aspects of Africa. The word "forest" is used instead of "jungle" and each of Africa's diverse cultural groups can be called by their individual names, such as the Yoruba people.

At Home Ideas: As children grow, they become increasingly interested in their roots. A very young child may have a difficult time comprehending information about his or her ancestry. You can, however, point out a few of the different countries your child's ancestors are from, along with exploring past and present aspects of these cultures. Your child's elderly relatives and your public library are great resources. This will help increase your child's self-identity, and sense of pride in cultural tradition. Learning that our country is made up of a rainbow of diverse cultures may help prevent prejudice, and promote acceptance of and respect for others. We must instill values of kindness and respect in today's children to ensure a peaceful tomorrow.

If you are interested in responding to hunger in Africa and other parts of the world, here is one source:

Meals for Millions/Freedom from Hunger Foundation
1644 DaVinci Court
Davis, CA 95616

Anytime you would like to share information from a culture of Africa, or another culture (including your child's and/or your own), we welcome you to do so.

Sincerely,

ACTIVITY 10: Words from African Languages

Objectives: Appreciation for diverse languages, and discovering linguistic diversity within Africa.

Note: There are thousands of different languages spoken in Africa. Remember, as in any language, word usage and pronunciation can vary greatly from place to place. For example, a greeting in English in the United States may be any of the following, depending on many factors, including your age and where you live: "Hello," "Hi," "Howdy," "Hi-ya," or "Hey."

KISWAHILI: Kiswahili is spoken throughout Africa more than any other language.
jambo (JAHM boe): *hello*
mama (mah MAH): *mother*
baba (bah BAH): *father*
rafiki (ra FEE kee): *friend*

SETSWANA: A language which can be found in Botswana.
dumela (du MEH la): *hello to one person* (Must be said with a handshake.)
dumelang (du MEH lang): *hello to more than one person*
mme (mmeh): *mother*
rre (rolled "r" sound - rreh): *father*
ntate (n TAH tay): *another word for father*
tsala (TSAH lah): *friend*
tsala yame (TSAH lah YAH mee): *my friend*

KRIO: A language from Sierra Leone.
kushE (ku sheh): *hello to one person*
una kushE (OO na koo sheh): *hello to more than one person*
mama (mah MA): *mother*
papa (pah PAH): *father*
padi (pah DEE): *friend*
mi padi (mee pah DEE): *my friend*

YORUBA: A language from Nigeria.
màmá (mah mah): *mother*
bàbá (bah bah): *father*
oṛé (OR ray): *friend*
Bawo ni? (BA woe nee): a greeting similar to, *"How's it going?"*
There is no literal translation for, "Hello."

Tips: Words from other languages can be incorporated within music, stories, and conversations with your group of children on a daily basis. Remember to mention which language the word is from. Studies of the human brain have shown that it is much easier for a person to learn a foreign language prior to age ten. See Appendix for further resources of African languages.

ACTIVITY 11: Foods Grown in Africa - Peanut Soup Recipe

Objectives: Cooking, math, language, and integration of multi-ethnic foods.

Ingredients:
- 2 tablespoons onion
- 2 tablespoons butter or margarine
- 2 tablespoons flour
- 1 cup chunky peanut butter
- 2 cups hot water
- 6 cups milk
- 1 low sodium chicken bouillon cube

Preparation: Saute onion with butter or margarine. Stir in flour. Mix together peanut butter, hot water, and milk. Add onions, cook over low heat, and stir until smooth. Add bouillon cube. Heat slowly, stirring often until hot and bouillon is dissolved.

Serves 12 children.

Ask the Children: Does everyone in Africa eat peanut soup? What is your favorite food? Does everyone in this city/country eat your favorite food?

Tips: Foods to introduce to your children may include: mangos, papayas, plantains, and coconuts. Please don't limit offering new recipes and foods from other countries to only those times you are teaching about them. Many grocery stores have mangos available by late May or early June, and they are generally available throughout the summer. Papayas may be more difficult to find, but a large grocery store will usually special order them for you. See Appendix for more recipes from Africa.

ACTIVITY 12: Sign Language African Animals Book

Objective: Sign language skills, familiarity with African animals, and fostering a love of books.

Materials:
- African wildlife stickers (See Appendix for purchasing information or make your own)
- five halved pieces of construction paper or large unlined index cards
- a stapler

Preparation: Order or make your stickers. Make each child an empty book by stapling together pieces of construction paper or index cards.

Procedure: Give each child an empty book. Have them place one African animal sticker on each page of their books. If they are interested in writing the name of each animal on their pages, write down the names of each animal and attach the corresponding sticker next to it and hang it where the children can see it to copy the letters. Allow them to use the writing instruments of their choice.

Now you can play Sign Language games with the children and help them learn the Signs for the animals. For example, Sign an animal and ask them to guess which animal you are Signing. Then have the children show their friends the Signs to guess which animal is being Signed. After the children know how to Sign all of the animals in their books they can take them home to teach their families these new Sign Language skills.

Ask the Children: If you went to a city in Africa, would you see large animals? Where? (In a zoo.) Are there only animals living in Africa, or do people live there too?

Tips: Animals such as giraffes, gorillas, lions and elephants are mostly found on a small number of game reserves and parks which you can describe to the children as "huge zoos" with natural habitats.

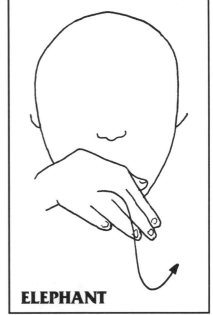

ELEPHANT

ACTIVITY 13: Pretend to Be Your Favorite Animal from Africa

Objectives: Creative movement and large muscle skills.

Procedure: Ask the children to choose an African animal which they would like to pretend to be. Then explain to them that these animals live on reserves which are special, large, outdoor zoos. Ask the children what type of noise will they make as they pretend to be this animal. How will they walk or move like this animal?

Tips: To incorporate Sign Language skills in this activity, you may wish to Sign an animal and have the children figure out which one it is. Then, have the class pretend to be that animal until you Sign a different animal.

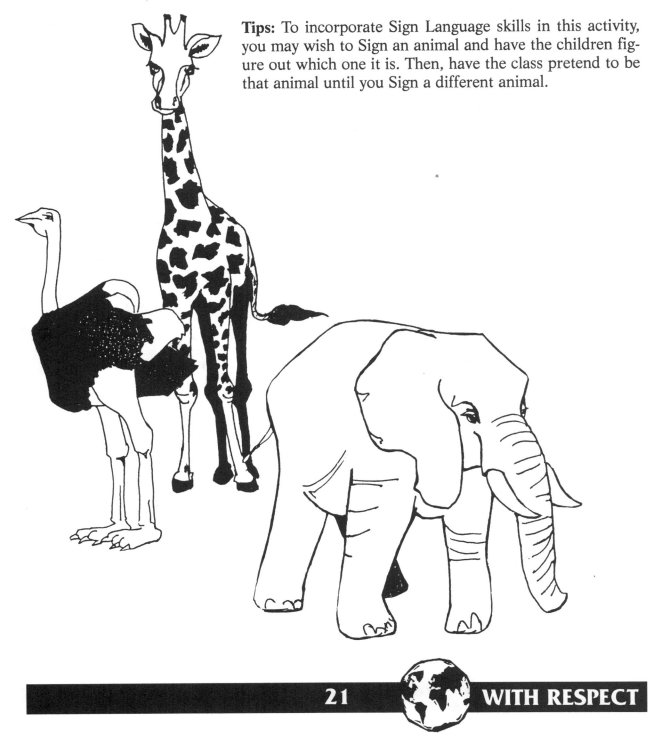

ACTIVITY 14: What's My Climate?

Objectives: Cognitive and sensory skills.

Materials:
- clothing for hot weather and cold or snowy weather
- white sheets (which can be wrapped around the head, held over the face, and draped over the body in desert regions to repel blowing sands)
- a clear plastic jar or glass half-filled with sand

Procedure: Dress in clothes which would be worn in hot weather. Tell the children, "I am pretending to live somewhere in Africa. Do you think the weather is hot or cold there?"

Next, put on clothes for cold weather and ask the above question once again.

Then, put on sheet-like clothing. Drape it over your head and face. Ask the children why they think you would be wearing clothes like this. This is not an easy one! Then pass around a plastic jar or glass of sand. Tell the children that in desert regions of the world (including parts of Africa) where there are people living, the sand often blows in the wind. How would these clothes be helpful in blowing sand? How would these clothes be helpful in a hot climate with a lot of sunshine?

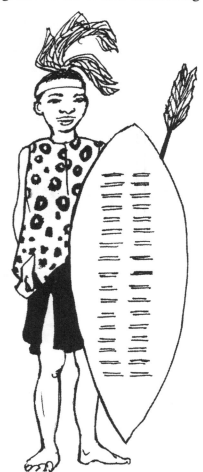

Mention to the children that there are also other reasons for which people may wear clothes that cover their faces and body, such as religious purposes.

Ask the Children: Does every person in the world who wears clothes which are like this live in a sandy desert? Have you ever seen anyone with clothes similar to this in your town? Is it okay for you to dress differently from other people? Is it okay for other people to dress differently from you?

ACTIVITY 15: City Life/Village Life Cards(Differences)

Objectives: Cognitive skills, and exploring cultural diversity in Africa.

Materials: *City Life/Village Life Cards with the following scenes:*
- *Getting water:* from a faucet in a city and from a well in a village
- *Music/dance:* a radio in a city and musicians in a village
- *Food:* a grocery checkout counter in a city and fishing or farming in a village
- *Home:* an apartment building in a city and a home made from natural materials in a village
- *Brushing teeth:* with a toothbrush in a city and using a finger or stick in a village

Preparation: Photocopy and cut out the cards. You may wish to enlarge each one as you photocopy it. Use heavy paper so that the cards will be more durable.

Procedure: Gather the children together on the floor. Hold up the cards one at a time and ask the children what is happening in each picture. Then have them guess whether each card depicts life in an African village or a city.

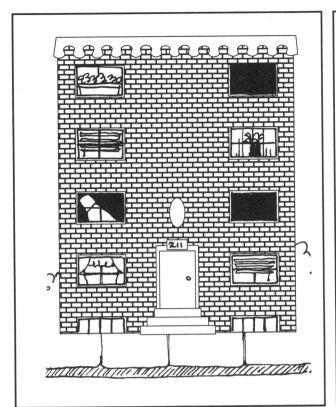

ACTIVITY 16: City People/Village People Pantomime (Similarities)

Objectives: Visual and cognitive skills, recognition of humanistic similarities, and dramatic play.

Procedure: Act out or have the children take turns acting out each of the humanistic similarities listed below between city people and village people, and allow the children to guess what is being pantomimed.

Some Humanistic Similarities:
Eating
Working
Sleeping
Dancing
Fear
Joy
Sorrow
Anger
Love
Singing
Playing

Ask the Children: How are we the same as and different from people who live elsewhere in the world? How are you different from one another? Stress the common bond of humanness.

Tips: You may wish to add your own ideas to this list. You can also have the children name other similarities that are more difficult to pantomime (i.e. learning, wishing, respecting, etc.)

ACTIVITY 17: Gourds

Objectives: Teaching children about science and gardening, introduction to multicultural music, instruments, and rhythm.

Materials: Locate and purchase a cekere for your class. A cekere (shay kah ray) is one of the gourd instruments which can be found in many parts of Africa. See the Appendix for gourd purchasing information. In mid to late October, gourds are often available where pumpkins are sold. For each child, buy a small gourd with a nice handle-shape near the stem.

Preparation: Making cekeres is much too complicated for preschoolers. Therefore, you can have the children allow their gourds to dry during the winter months making certain that the gourd is allowed to freeze during that time.

Procedure: After the gourds are dry they will make wonderful shakers which the children can use as rhythm instruments. The shakers can be scraped with steel wool and painted with acrylics or other paints. Tell the children that gourds are made into musical instruments as well as other things - including containers, ladles, and masks - in Africa and in many other parts of the world.

Tips: If you cannot find a cekere to show your class, you may wish to obtain a simple rattle or some maracas to let the children experiment with simple rhythms. You may wish to open a gourd and save the seeds to plant your own gourds the following spring. Start seeds indoors, set pots outdoors to acclimate them, then move them outdoors, planting each one in a mound of dirt about 10" high x 10" across.

ACTIVITY 18: Two African Folktales as told by Michael Oladejo Afolayan

Objectives: Introduction to multicultural storytelling, listening and language skills.

Michael's home is Nigeria and he has a doctorate in African Studies. These folktales can be heard throughout Africa, and are common among the Yoruba people. For Michael, who is Yoruba, storytelling was an important part of childhood. His father told the family stories each evening before bedtime. In keeping with the tradition of storytelling, please read these stories to yourself and **tell** them to the children.

The Old Man and His Son

Here's a story about an old man and his son. This was a long, long, long time ago in a village where there were no cars, there were no bikes, there were no airplanes, and there were no trains. It was difficult for people to travel. Wouldn't it be difficult to travel? But, there was something they used for traveling. It was a donkey. A donkey looks like a small horse with long ears. So, one day, the old man told his son, "My son, I am going to travel tomorrow. I am going to visit my relatives in another village."

The son said, "Oh, Daddy, I want to go with you."

And the father said, "Okay, you can go with me."

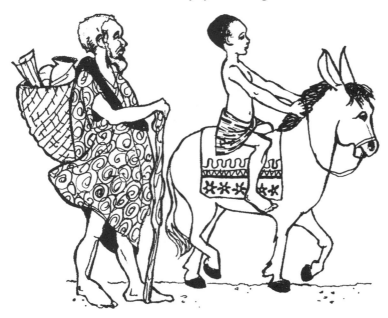

So, the morning came and they were ready to go. The son packed his things and the father packed his things, and they put everything on top of the donkey. Then the old man told his son, "I want you to walk for a while. I will be on the donkey and you walk beside me. And when you're tired or you've had enough exercise, I'll put you on top of the donkey." The son said, "Sure! Let's go."

So they started their journey. The donkey is a very slow animal. So they started going slowly, and slowly, and slowly, and slowly. They got to a village. And when people of this village saw them, they said, "What?! Old man, you must be wicked. You are sitting on the donkey, you put your things on top of the donkey, and your poor boy is walking? That's not fair!"

And the old man said, "Oh, I am sorry. I am sorry." Then he said, "Okay my son, come and sit on the donkey."

So his son sat on the donkey. The old man then jumped down from the donkey, and they continued with their journey. I told you how the donkey walks...slowly, and slowly, and slowly, and slowly. And pretty soon they got to another village. People of this village saw them and said, "What?! Old man, are you stupid? Your son is sitting on the donkey, you put your things on the donkey, and you are walking?! You are stupid."

And the old man said, "Oh, I am sorry, I am sorry." Then he said, "Okay, let me sit on the donkey."

So the old man sat on the donkey, and his son sat on the donkey, they put their things on top of the donkey, and they continued with their journey. And I told you how the donkey walks...slowly, and slowly, and slowly, and slowly. And soon they got to another village, people of this village saw them and said, "What?! You people must be wicked. You, old man are sitting on the donkey. Your son is sitting on the donkey, and you put your heavy things on top of the donkey. Do you want to kill that poor animal?"

And the old man said, "Oh, I am sorry. I am sorry." Then he said, "Okay my son, jump down from the donkey."

So the son jumped down from the donkey, the old man jumped down from the donkey, and they took down their things from the donkey. And they continued with their journey. I told you how the donkey walks...slowly, and slowly, and slowly, and slowly. And very soon they came to another village. And guess what the people said then? They said, "What?! You people are stupid! Are you fools? You are walking by the donkey, your son is walking by the donkey, you took your things off the donkey, and your donkey is walking empty? What are donkeys for?"

And the old man looked at his son and said, "Uh-oh my son. What can we do?"

And the son said, "I don't know."

And then–ooh!–the donkey started talking and said, "Well, why don't you just do what you think is right?"

And the old man said, "Oh, the donkey said we should do what we think is right."

So, the old man sat on the donkey, the son sat on the donkey, and whenever they got to another village and the people said, "What?!"

They would just look back at them and smile.

So, they continued with their journey, and they were happy thereafter, got to where they wanted to go, and came back to their little village. So that is the end of the story.

Moral: Do what *you* think is right.

This story is one that you can hear people tell everywhere in Africa. The Yoruba people call the donkey, "Kete" (ke'ta ke'ta). "Kete" means something that is slow. In other places they have different names for the same animal.

The Turtle, the Hippo, and the Elephant

Do you know the biggest animal on land in Africa and anywhere in the world? The elephant. Do you know the biggest animal in the rivers? The hippo. Do you know one of the smallest animals? The turtle.

Now, let me tell you the story about the turtle, the hippo and the elephant. You see, it's not good to boast. Everyday the elephant would go about in the forest boasting, "I am very powerful. I am very powerful. No animal is as powerful as I am."

One day, the elephant saw the turtle and said, "Turtle, get out of here! I am the biggest animal and nobody's as powerful as I am!"

And the turtle said, "Oh, are you sure? You know, I may be more powerful than you are."

The elephant laughed and said, "You are kidding! Not you! You, small turtle? No way! You have no power!"

So the turtle walked away and went to the river to bathe and swim. Then he saw the hippo, the biggest animal in the river. Hippo was also boasting, "I'm the biggest animal in the river. I'm the most powerful. I can eat any fish I want. I am big!" And then he saw the turtle swimming and he said, "Turtle! You'd better get out of here! I'm going to eat you!"

The turtle said, "Don't eat me! You know, it's not good to boast when you have power. I may actually be more powerful than you are."

And the hippo laughed and said, "What?! You, little turtle, are more powerful than I am? You are kidding me! I will eat you!"

The turtle walked away. And then do you know what he did? He went to buy a BIG rope – a very STRONG rope, and he went back to the river and said, "Hippo, do you want to compete with me? I can pull you. I will be on the top of the hill. You stay in the river and pull me, and I will pull you. Whoever is stronger will pull the other one out of wherever they are."

The hippo said, "Me? You are joking. You and I will pull? Okay. Where's the rope?"

So, the turtle tied the rope around the hippo's neck and the turtle took the rope to the other side of the hill. Then he went to the elephant and said, "Elephant, you were boasting before. Here I come. Do you want to pull me?"

The elephant said, "Pull?"

The turtle said, "Tie this rope around your neck, and I will go to the other side of the hill. When I say, 'Pull!' Then you start to pull. If you are stronger than I am, then you will be able to pull me. If I am stronger than you, then I will be able to pull you."

And so, do you know what the turtle did? He went to the top of the hill and hid there. Meanwhile, the rope was tied around the elephant's neck and the other end was tied around the hippo's neck. So, the turtle said, "P – U – L – L!"

As soon as he said, "Pull," the elephant pulled, and the hippo pulled. They thought they were pulling the turtle, but actually, who were they pulling? The elephant and the hippo were pulling each other! So, the turtle said, "Pull!" again, and they continued to pull, and pull, and pull, and they did it day and night, and day and night, and day and night for 7 days and 7 nights.

Then on the 8th day, they started to get very tired. The elephant said, "Let me go and check. I have to go and see. Can the turtle be so strong? I am so ashamed of myself."

So instead of pulling, the elephant and the hippo decided to go up the hill to see the other side and see how the turtle could be so strong. Soon both the elephant and the hippo found out who they were pulling. When they got to the top of the hill, the elephant said, "What?! It's the hippo I've been pulling?"

And the hippo said, "What?! It's the elephant I've been pulling? I thought I'd been pulling the turtle!"

And so, both the elephant and the hippo were ashamed of themselves. The turtle started laughing at them. Then the turtle said, "You've learned your lesson. Don't look down on the little ones. The little ones are also very strong."

Moral: Even the very small have strength and wisdom.

Tips: Encourage children to come up with their own morals, as well. One story may have many different meanings for different listeners.

  **WITH RESPECT**

ACTIVITY 19: Song of Africa

Objectives: Global awareness, exploring Africa's cultural diversity, music and rhythm skills.

Africa

Refrain:
Africa, Africa, Africa, Africa.
Africa, Africa is very far away from here,
is very far away.

Verses:
In Africa there are cities -
with people and buildings galore.
The people drive lots of cars there,
and buy their things at the stores.

In villages people are busy -
they work and play and talk.
The people don't need a car there,
they ride in a boat or walk.

In Africa there are places -
where lions and zebras roam free.
There are boa constrictors,
gorillas and chimpanzees.

Tips: This song can be found on the audio cassette, *Music With Respect*, Volume 1P-2P. Please see the Appendix for more information on this and other cassettes featuring African song and dance.

Be sure to include many styles and types of music from different parts of the world in your teaching regularly. Contact your public library for available African music. If there is not a diverse selection, place a written request to the library Board of Directors for purchasing additional musical cassettes. Explain in writing how great the need is to offer a vast variety of African music. A continent the size of Africa should be represented with more than one audio cassette! Please make written requests for other needed multicultural musical cassettes as well. See **Activity 76: Drawing to Various Music and Sounds,** for ideas to use throughout these multicultural units.

UNIT THREE
Mexican Cultural Aspects

MEXICO

UNIT THREE: Mexican Cultural Aspects
Introduction

When thinking of Mexico, one often thinks of things such as sombreros, piñatas or mariachi bands. Each of these things is a very real and important part of Mexican culture. Yes, even sombreros! The Mexican Hat Dance, Mexico's national dance, is still performed, and gauchos (cowboys) wear sombreros (hats with large brims) at rodeos to help prevent injury in case of a fall from a horse. I have read numerous articles and books which imply that to show children items such as those previously mentioned is "stereotyping" people from Mexico. If a teacher were to expose the children only to sombreros, pinatas and mariachi bands, there would be a problem. However, if these things are introduced along with explanations, as well as many other diverse cultural aspects, it can be wonderful. Virtually all of the many people I have spoken with and/or worked with from other countries do not want their cultures to be hidden. They are deeply proud and wish to retain their own cultures, including language, traditions, celebrations, religion, foods, music, and dance. Many people wish to share information about their cultures not only to educate, but also to ease cultural and racial barriers, and to alleviate fears of unfamiliar cultural differences. Subsequently, sincere interest and respect for other cultures can occur.

After the Spanish invasion of Mexico, many of the Native Americans of Mexico inter-married with Spanish people. These people who are of both Spanish and Native American descent are known as Mestizos. There are many Native American peoples existing today in Mexico, many of which live in their own villages each with their own distinct language and customs. Poverty has drawn many of these people to large cities where they can find work, often selling handmade crafts or hand grown foods. Despite the Spanish invasion, many of the Native American peoples of Mexico, such as the Aztecs and Mayas, have retained some of their historical artifacts including huge temples and pyramids.

Although Spanish is the primary language spoken in Mexico, it is important to remember that it is not Mexico's only language. It is also important to know that Spanish is spoken not only in Mexico, but in many other countries including parts of the United States, such as in communities with large Hispanic populations. The Spanish language varies linguistically throughout the United States and within other countries, including Mexico.

A Note on Mexican American People: One of the important things to remember about Mexican American people is that they are not all newly arrived to the United States. Many generations of Mexican families have been in America for hundreds of years; therefore, not all of them speak Spanish. Some Mexican Americans speak only Spanish among themselves and in their homes, and consider Spanish their first language. We must respect a person's right to retain his or her own language. After all, English was not the first or "native" language of the United States. Ask a Native American person.

Once more, I wish to stress that this book be a seed for a growing multicultural curriculum. People, not just books, are the absolute best way to share other cultures with your children.

UNIT THREE: Mexican Cultural Aspects (Letter to Parents)

Date:

Dear Parents:

This week our primary unit will focus upon cultural aspects of Mexico. If you or someone in your family is from Mexico, we welcome you to visit and share your culture with us. If you have visited Mexico and have any art pieces, books, or other interesting items that you would like the children to see, we would be delighted to borrow them or have you show them to us.

We will be finding out a bit about Mexico and its many languages. We will learn some words of the primary language, Spanish, as well as a few words of the Aztec language, Nahuatl. There are many other Native American languages such as Mixteco, Maya, Zapateco and Otomi (to name just a few) spoken in Mexico by the many different groups of Native American people who live there. You may wish to use some of the words from the following page with your child.

As in each of the multicultural units we do together, we will encourage interest, curiosity, and respect for diversity among peoples and places.

At Home Ideas: If you know of a good Mexican restaurant or recipe for a Mexican entree, this would be a perfect time to enjoy a Mexican meal with your child. The majority of food served in large chains of Mexican restaurants in the United States is quite unlike that served in Mexico. To taste authentic food, you can locate a restaurant that is owned and operated by people who are Mexican American.

When visiting the library, you may wish to borrow records or tapes of music from Mexico. It is important to offer your child the opportunity to hear music from other countries not only this week, but regularly! Along with choosing music pertaining to this unit, you may also wish to select a few books on the topic to reinforce what your child is learning and to add a variety of information.

Once again, whether your family's background is of one culture or several cultures, we welcome you to visit and share a story, a craft, a song, or another aspect of your culture. Helping children develop an awareness of cultural diversity will promote their interest in and respect for the differences among people and cultures. With your help, this future adult generation may be able to live in a society in which many cultures can exist peacefully.

Sincerely,

ACTIVITY 20: Words from the Spanish Language

Objectives: Knowledge of and respect for the use of other languages.

Mejico (MEH hee ko): *Mexico*

platano (PLAH tah no): *banana*

pasas (PAH sahs): *raisins*

manzana (man ZAH nah): *apple*

buenos dias (BWEH nos DEE us): *good day*

por favor (POOR fa VOOR): *please*

hola (OH lah): *hello*

adios (ah dee OHS): *goodbye*

amigo (ah ME go): *friend*

gracias (GRA syus): *thank you*

siesta (see YES ta): *afternoon nap – An old tradition which is no longer practiced by most Mexican people today.*

!viva! (VEE vah): *hurrah, long life, shout of acclamation*

agua (AH gwa): *water*

uno: *one*

dos: *two*

tres: *three*

cuatro: *four*

cinco: *five*

seis: *six*

siete: *seven*

ocho: *eight*

nueve: *nine*

diez: *ten*

ACTIVITY 21: Words in Nahuatl (Aztec Language)

Objectives: Awareness of cultural and linguistic diversity within Mexico.

Titocnihuan: *We are friends.*

Conētl: *child*

Chōca: *cry or weep*

Tips: Include some of these and other foreign words when speaking with the children regularly. You don't have to limit using foreign words to the weeks when that particular country is the primary unit. It is important that you ask the children what the word means and which language the word is from. Give frequent reminders. Tell the children that many people who live in the United States and many other countries speak Spanish as their primary language.

WITH RESPECT

ACTIVITY 22: A Song or Poem

Objectives: Familiarity with Spanish language, music and rhythm skills.

In Mexico

In Mexico, in Mexico,
    the people speak Espanol.
       Oh Mexico, Oh Mexico,
I can learn Spanish too.

Verses:
In Spanish, people say "Amigo." (ah MEE go)
In English, people say "Friend."
In Spanish, people say "Hola." (OH lah)
In English, people say,"Hi."
(Return to chorus)

In Spanish, people say "Gluten." (GLOO tin)
In English, people say "Glue."
In Spanish, people say "Pintura." (peen TOOH rah)
In English, people say "Paint."
(Return to chorus)

In Spanish, people say "Gracias." (GRAH syus)
In English, people say "Thanks."
In Spanish, people say "Adios." (ah DEE ose)
In English, they say "Goodbye."

Tips: Although Spanish is the primary language spoken, many other languages exist in Mexico, as well. This song can be found on the audio cassette, *Music With Respect, Volume 1-2P*. Please see the Appendix for purchasing information.

ACTIVITY 23: Guiros (WEER roes) ~ Gourd or Wooden Instruments

Objectives: Introduction to multicultural instruments, music, rhythm, and movement.

Materials:
- pieces of corrugated cardboard with corrugation exposed
- wooden dowels or unsharpened pencils
- a real guiro

Procedure: Have the children listen to music from Mexico. Then they can slide their dowels across the corrugated cardboard ridges as rhythm instruments to play along. You may wish to include other rhythm instruments such as maracas. (See the following activity.)

Tips: You might want to have the children play their makeshift guiros to some African music, as well. Let the children know that African music and rhythms have had great influence upon music in certain regions of Mexico such as Vera Cruz, along with many other parts of the world. See the Appendix for information on how to find authentic Mexican music.

ACTIVITY 24: Making Maracas

Objectives: Creative expression, music and rhythm.

Materials for each child:
- a plastic container with a lid
- different types of objects to place in the containers such as salt, rice, macaroni, sand, pebbles, buttons, or milk bottle lids
- a large spoon for scooping
- colored masking tape (available from Creative Thoughts and Surplus, see Appendix) **or** regular masking tape
- acrylic paints and brushes

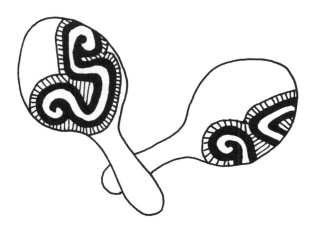

Procedure: Give each child a container, a spoon, and a substance of their choice to place inside, such as pebbles or sand. Have them scoop the sand or other substance into a container, place the lids on their containers, and wind tape around them to keep them tightly closed. Then the children can decorate their maracas with acrylic paints if desired. Be sure to show the children real maracas made from dried gourds which contain pebbles or other small items.

Tips: Due to the messiness of this activity, you may wish to do it outdoors. Salt can damage plants and concrete, so use caution if salt is used. You may wish to try some of the previous musical activities in this unit with the children's maracas. Or, for a day, have the children shake their maracas when they raise their hands.

ACTIVITY 25: Sound Matching Game

Objectives: Auditory discrimination, listening and sorting skills.

Materials: Several of the maracas made in the previous activity.

Procedure: Have the children try to match the maracas according to sound. For example, they can sort all of the containers with sand in them by placing them in a group, and all of the containers with pebbles in them in another group.

Tips: If you are finished using the maracas for different activities, you may want to take them apart to use the containers for later activities. After the children sort the instruments, open them up and see how well they guessed. Save one or two maracas, however, to keep in the classroom for the children to play with.

ACTIVITY 26: Weaving

Objectives: Fine-motor skills, and appreciation for multicultural crafts.

Materials:
- a paper grocery bag for each child
- scissors
- many colorful paper strips approximately 12" x 3"

Preparation: Open the paper bags. Cut out the blank, back side of each bag and discard the rest. Draw lines 3" apart from the opening to the first fold. Fold the bags in half and make long cuts in them on the lines, leaving about 2" uncut around the sides and top of the bag.

Procedure: The children can weave the colorful strips of paper in and out of the cuts in the paper bag piece. They may wish to make small cuts all around the outer edges of their weavings.

Tips: Weaving is still practiced by many different ethnic groups in Mexico as well as worldwide. To obtain weaving or handcrafts from Mexico, look in the Appendix for phone numbers and addresses.

WITH RESPECT

ACTIVITY 27: Send a Message with Mural Art

Objectives: Creative expression, cooperative social and communication skills.

Materials:
- tempera paints (thick, dripless consistency)
- paint brushes
- paper
- rags
- smocks or clothes that can get dirty

Preparation: The children can brainstorm a message they would like to send to their parents, families, and community by way of mural painting. The message may be something such as, "I love my family" or "Monsters aren't real." Allow each child to choose his or her own colors and way of expressing this message through painting. You may find it easier to place the paper on the floor and have the children paint there. After the paint is dry, the mural(s) can be hung. Invite parents and families to see the murals. You may also ask local store owners, or your own principal, if you can display the mural(s) to the public. Libraries and supermarkets are another venue you can ask to display the children's art work.

Tips: One cooperative mural can be made, or each child can make their own. The late Mexican muralist, Diego Rivera is one of many whose brilliant work remains world famous. Rivera's work often reflected political messages such as national independence.

ACTIVITY 28: Mosaic Art

Objectives: Tactile exploration and creative expression.

Materials:
- colorful aquarium gravel **or** hardened tempera paints (* see below)
- a small piece of heavy paper for each child
- glue
- a hole puncher
- pieces of yarn or ribbon

Preparation: Entire interior and exterior walls of beautiful stone mosaic can be found in public places throughout Mexico. Here are a few suggestions for doing mosaics with young children. You may want to go to your local or school library and ask for books with pictures of mosaics, or murals from the preceding activity to show the children before they begin. This is another messy activity best done outside or on the floor.

Procedure: Allow the children to cover their papers with glue. Then they can place pieces of gravel or hardened paint pieces on the glue. After the mosaics have dried, you can punch a hole in the corner and tie a piece of yarn or ribbon through them so the mosaics can be hung. The yarn makes it easier to hang the mosaics since they can become quite heavy. Send these home with the children in bags, since they can be messy to transport. Rather than buying bags, please reuse them.

*To make hardened tempera paints: Mix powdered tempera paints in large shallow containers with water. Add corn starch to thicken the paint slightly. Allow the paints to air dry and solidify. Pound the bottoms of the containers onto a table top in order to break the hardened paint into small pieces.

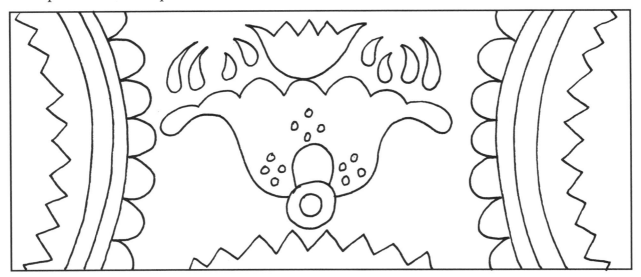

WITH RESPECT

ACTIVITY 29: Piñata Suggestions

Objectives: Gross and fine-motor coordination, introduction to multicultural celebrations.

Materials:
- a large balloon
- newspaper, shredded into strips
- flour and water mixed into a paste
- tissue paper
- a wiffle ball bat, or something to break the piñata with
- candy or treat bags for each child
- *optional:* eye covers (See Activity 57: Touching with Covered Hands, for instructions on how to make these.)

Preparation: You may wish to purchase a piñata or you can make one by blowing up a large balloon, and hanging it upside down by a string. Then dip shredded newspaper strips into a thick paste of flour and water, and remove the excess paste by sliding the strips of newspaper between two of your fingers. Then place each strip of newspaper on the balloon. To add a decorative touch, use layers of tissue paper strips dipped in the flour mixture over the newspaper layers. Allow the piñata to dry for several days. Cut a hole in the top, and pop the balloon. Have the children paint the piñata as a group project. After it dries, fill it with the treat bags. Remind the children that, traditionally, piñatas are filled with candy and small toys.

Procedure: When the piñata is completely dry, pick a time for the children to take turns trying to break it. Make sure that everyone gets a turn. You might also want to play some festive Mexican music in the background, or coordinate this with another activity in the unit. For example, ask a question about Mexico and if the class gets the answer right, the next child gets a turn.

Ask the Children: Does everyone in Mexico make or use piñatas? (No.) Do people who live in Mexico celebrate and have parties every day? (No.) What else do people do in Mexico? (Work, play, eat meals, sleep, etc.)

Tips: Making piñatas with children is not a new idea. Piñatas involve both surprise and candy, two things most all children love. You may wish to alter the tradition a little by placing a small sandwich bag filled with healthy treats such as low-salt crackers, raisins, or dry cereal, and stickers for each child into the piñata labeled with the children's names. This alleviates some of the pushing and greed that can occur during the breaking of the piñata.

ACTIVITY 30: Field Trip - Mexican Restaurant

Objectives: Appreciation for cultural diversity, and exposure to local businesses and professions.

Preparation: Telephone the manager of a Mexican restaurant for information on whether the restaurant has authentic Mexican decor and food. If so, set up an appointment for your group of children to come for a tour. When visiting restaurants with your children, be sure that they are not brought into a kitchen during food preparation hours.

Bring a camera, and request permission from the manager to take photographs as mementos for the children. You may want to take a photo of the manager with your children, and enclose the photo with the thank you note you send.

ACTIVITY 31: Tortillas

Objectives: Appreciation for multi-ethnic foods and eating utensils.

Preparation: It is important for children to understand that not everyone in the world uses knives, forks, and spoons. Whether it's hands, chopsticks, a vegetable, or a tortilla, periodically allow the children opportunities to try different eating utensils.

Tortillas are a very important food in Mexico. They can be used to wrap foods in, such as an enchilada, and can be used as eating utensils (for stews) when rolled up. Try several ways of eating tortillas with the children. Beans and corn are also important foods in Mexican cuisine.

  **WITH RESPECT**

ACTIVITY 32: Special Visitors - A Mexican Dance Group

Objectives: Exposure to multicultural music and dance.

Preparation: Try to locate a Mexican dance group which would either allow your group of children to come and see them perform, or have the dancers visit your group. If you have a particularly small amount of children, you may wish to combine your group with another small group to have a larger audience.

Call a local dance studio in your yellow pages for information, and check your public library listing of local ethnic organizations, many of which are dance groups. Request that the children be allowed to see the dancers in both their special dance clothing as well as their contemporary clothing. This will help the children to see that past heritage and customs can be celebrated, but traditional clothing is worn mostly for celebrations and dance demonstrations.

Ask the Children: Does everyone in Mexico dance? What does your family do to celebrate?

Tips: On the following page is the sheet music for The Mexican Hat Dance. Children will enjoy dancing to the music.

THE MEXICAN HAT DANCE

Traditional

Partners face each other, left shoulder to left shoulder. Beginning right, step from heel to toe 8 times. Turn to face opposite direction (right shoulder to left shoulder) and repeat. Repeat action, facing opposite direction (left shoulder to left shoulder). Repeat the action. Hook right elbows, left hands held high. Take 8 running steps, clapping on the eighth step. Repeat action. The movements are the same for boy and girl.

ACTIVITY 33: Mountains

Objectives: Earth science, fine-motor skills, and dramatic play.

Materials:
- clay
- cotton
- small branches from shrubs (found on the ground or trimmed carefully from shrubs by the teacher)
- a large piece of cardboard
- *optional:* small plastic animals (mountain goats, birds, etc.)

Procedure: Give each child some clay to play with freely. After allowing plenty of time for free play, ask each child to shape his or her clay into a mountain. Cotton can be added to the tops for snow. Ask the children if they think trees would grow at the very cold peaks of mountains. Then allow them to add branches for trees and plastic animals if desired. Place all of the children's clay mountains onto a large piece of cardboard. Ask the children to place their mountains in a circle. In the center of the mountains you or the children can draw a city with roads and buildings or make one out of building blocks. You can add props such as small toy cars, signs, or boxes for buildings. Tell the children that Mexico City, the capital of Mexico, is surrounded by mountains.

Geography of Mexico: Eighty percent of Mexico is covered by mountains which were formed by volcanoes. The highest point of Mexico is the volcano Orizaba, which is 18,855 feet high. Due to the bodies of water that surround Mexico, the climate is hot and humid along the coastal areas, and hot and dry towards the north. The land around the coastal areas, volcanoes, and rivers is fertile and productive.

Ask the Children: Is Mexico the only country that has mountains?

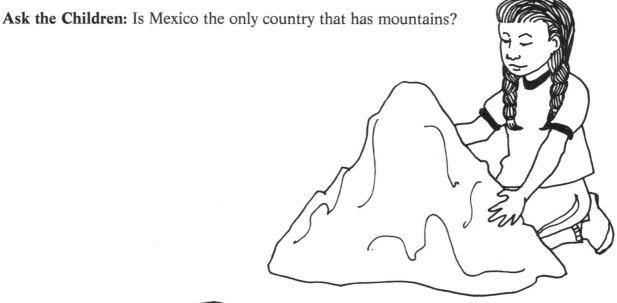

UNIT FOUR
French Cultural Aspects

FRANCE

WITH RESPECT

UNIT FOUR: French Cultural Aspects
Introduction

France is one of the few countries to have very few negative stereotypes associated with it. In fact most of the stereotypes are such as these: French people are wealthy; French people are all very fashionable; French people prepare and eat gourmet foods at every meal; All French people are artistically and musically creative.

In reality, in France as in every country, there are wealthy people and there are poor people. There are people who live in large cities and people who farm. Stereotyping or categorizing in a positive way can be as destructive and inaccurate as negative stereotyping.

Since the Statue of Liberty is so interesting to children, it would be a good time to mention the fact that the statue was a gift to the United States from France.

France has an ethnically diverse population which includes people who are not only originally from France, but also many other parts of the world, including: Italy, Portugal, Africa, and Southeast Asia. French is the official language, although there are other dialects spoken. Provençal is spoken in Provence, Briton is spoken in Brittany, as well as Flemish, Terman, Basque, and Catalan in other regions.

UNIT FOUR: French Cultural Aspects (Letter to Parents)

Date:

Dear Parents:

This week our primary unit will be "French Cultural Aspects." First, we will be learning songs and poems about counting in French. See the following page for some French words we will be using, along with the numbers in French from one to ten.

We will taste crepes (and find out that french fries aren't really French) and other traditional French cuisine. Several activities explore the diversity within France, such as the differences between city and country living. We will also explore the similarities between France and our country. We will see what the Eiffel Tower looks like and make special sculptures of our own. We will also do some activities related to ballet, the sport of bicycle racing, pantomime, and Impressionist painting. By the way, the original French Impressionist artists were laughed at by critics, but persevered with their work - now those late artists are world acclaimed. We will talk about how it feels to be laughed at, and the value of believing in yourself.

I would like to invite you again to share any experiences, stories, or crafts with our class that pertain to France. This would also be an opportune time to rent one of the many brilliant French films with subtitles to watch while your child is playing. You might be surprised at how quickly your child picks up foreign languages at this impressionable age.

Sincerely,

ACTIVITY 34: Words from the French Language

Objectives: Appreciation of another language, linguistic and pronunciation skills.

Note: There are many words in the English language which are French, such as bouquet, cafe, restaurant, and menu. French is spoken in countries other than France, such as in parts of Canada. Canadian French is quite different from the French spoken in France. Although French is the primary language, there are other languages spoken in France, such as Brittany, an ancient Celtic language, and Basque. It is best to hear French spoken to learn how to pronounce words correctly.

Français (Frahn SAY): *French*

bonjour (bohn ZJUER): *hello*

ça va? (sah VAH?): *How's it going*

oui (wee): *yes*

au revoir (aw rih VWAHR): *good bye*

maman (mah mahn): *mother*

papa (pah pa): *father*

mémé (may may): *grandma*

pépé (pay pay): *grandpa*

Je t'aime (zjeuh TEHM): *I love you*

un (ehn): *one*

deux (deuh): *two*

trois (twaa): *three*

quatre (cat trer): *four*

cinq (sank): *five*

six (seese): *six*

sept (set): *seven*

huit (wheat): *eight*

neuf (neuff): *nine*

dix (deese): *ten*

ACTIVITY 35: Ballet

Objectives: Exposure to multicultural music and dance.

Preparation: Since ballet originated in France, this would be a wonderful time to visit a dance studio which has pre-ballet classes available for small children. Request that the children be allowed to visit and see a brief dance demonstration, and have a brief, simple lesson. Explain to the children that the words used to describe movements in ballet are mostly French words. Have the children listen as the dance teacher speaks these words.

Ask the Children: Where did ballet first begin? Are all people who live in France ballet dancers? (No.) Do people in countries other than France dance ballet now? (Yes.)

ACTIVITY 36: The French City Mouse and Country Mouse (Puppet Show)

Objectives: Appreciation for diverse lifestyles within France.

Materials:
- heavy paper
- scissors
- paint or markers
- popsicle sticks

Preparation: Photocopy the mouse puppets onto heavy paper, cut them out, color them, and glue them to sticks.

Puppet Show:

City Mouse: "I haven't seen my sister Georgette for so long. I must give her a call and invite her to see me here in the city." (On the phone), "Bonjour Georgette, it is your sister Brigitte. I miss you very much and wonder if you would like to visit me in the city?"

Country Mouse: "Yes, Brigitte. I would like to come to the city, and I would love to see you again!"

Georgette (the country mouse) drives her car until she comes to the city and spends hours in the traffic. Car horns honk and engines roar filling her ears with unfamiliar noise. Georgette arrives at Brigitte's apartment. She cannot figure out why the first door she knocks on is not Brigitte's home. The person who answers the door says, "Read the names on the mailboxes to see which apartment number your sister lives in. There are many, many different families living in this building."

Georgette arrives at Brigitte's door and knocks.

Country Mouse: "This is it. Apartment neuf (nine)."

City Mouse: "Georgette, I am so happy to see you." (They hug.) Wait until you see all of the wonderful things there are in the city. Tomorrow we will see the bike racers go by in the streets for the Tour de France. This is my dog, 'Babette'."

Country Mouse: "What a nice dog. I have a dog on my farm too."

The next day, they watch along the street as the bicycles go by.

Country Mouse: "Brigitte, it is fun to be in the city, but I do not like to try to drive my car when there are so many other cars that we can hardly move."

City Mouse: "Georgette, I will show you a faster way to travel in our city."

They buy tickets to ride the metro (underground railway).

Country Mouse: "Brigitte, this metro is like riding on a train under the ground. It surely is faster than trying to drive my car through traffic."

They stop and eat at a Chinese restaurant. "We do not have any restaurants near my home in the country, and I have never tasted Chinese food. This is wonderful! Would you like to come with me to visit my home in the country now?"

City Mouse: "Oui (yes), Georgette! I would like to see the country."

They drive in Georgette's car to the country and arrive at Georgette's home. When they arrive, Georgette takes Brigitte fishing. They catch some fish. Then they pick apples from the tree in Georgette's yard and lettuce and strawberries from her garden. Georgette prepares a meal of fish, crepes, fresh fruit to roll up in the crepes, and salad.

City Mouse: "Georgette, this food is so good! It is hard work to grow your own food, but it tastes delicious. I see you have a dog also. Is it a friendly dog? May I pet it?"

Country Mouse: "Go right ahead and pet her. She is a very nice dog."

City Mouse: "It has been wonderful to visit your country home, Georgette, but I must return home. I must work tomorrow. I am still a fire fighter. Do you still write books Georgette?"

Country Mouse: "Oui (yes), I do. I am expected to work tomorrow also, Brigitte. Thanks for showing me your city home."

City Mouse: "Thanks for showing me your country home."

Both mice were pleased to visit new places, but happy to live in their own homes.

Ask the Children: Would you like to live with Brigitte or Georgette? Can you think of some other things that are different in the city and in the country?

CITY MOUSE Puppet

COUNTRY MOUSE Puppet

ACTIVITY 37: French Counting Song

Objectives: Learning French numbers, counting, music, and rhythm skills.

Un, Deux, Trois

Refrain: Un, deux, trois,
quatre, cinq,
six, sept, huit, neuf, dix.

Verses: I can count to ten in French.
Now won't you try it with me?
I can count to ten in French.
Now won't you try it with me?   *(To refrain)*

You can count to ten in French.
I'm proud of you and me.
You can count to ten in French.
I'm proud of you and me.   *(To refrain)*

Tips: The first song can be found on the audio cassette, *Music With Respect, Volume 1-2P.*
Please see the Appendix for more information. The second song, and many others, can be
found in *Drama & Music: Creative Activities for Young Children* also in the Appendix.

Frere Jacques

ACTIVITY 38: Pantomime

Objectives: Visual observation skills, appreciation for multicultural art forms.

Materials: face paint if desired

Procedure: One of the greatest mimes in the world is the Frenchman, Marcel Marceau. Take turns with the children using only body language (no spoken language or sounds) and have the others guess what you are pantomiming. Pantomime games develop a child's ability to think and make responses, creatively linking concept to movement.

Here are a few suggestions to get you started:
- Riding a bicycle
- Hammering a nail
- Cleaning
- Taking a bath
- Picking flowers
- Rowing a boat
- Crying
- Laughing
- Sleeping
- Swimming
- Cooking
- Jumping rope
- Eating spaghetti
- Going to sleep

Tips: You may wish to tell an entire story. Have the children describe each of your actions as you do them. One other adult to help you would let you act out many different scenarios that are hard to act out alone. The children may have fun participating in this, as well.

ACTIVITY 39: Impressionist Style Painting

Objectives: Art appreciation, creative expression, and encouraging perseverance.

Materials:
- thick paint in soft colors
- several different types of materials other than brushes to paint with, such as small pieces of cotton, sponge, fabric, or scraps of scrunched newspaper

Preparation: Some copies of French Impressionist paintings. Consult your public librarian to see if they have paintings which can be borrowed. These are to be passed around the class or shown to the children briefly before the activity. Also check on books or encyclopedias of artwork featuring the work of artists such as Renoir, Monet, and Pissaro.

Procedure: Allow the children to use the cottonballs or other materials to dab the paint softly onto their papers. They may choose to vary from this technique, which is perfectly fine. If every child's piece of art looks the same, it's not art. If brushes are requested, please supply them.

Ask the Children: How does it feel to be laughed at or criticized? If someone has hurt our feelings, should we tell them how we feel? (Yes!)

Tips: The great French Impressionist artists were laughed at by critics when they began. Now their paintings are appreciated and admired around the world. Tell the children that believing in themselves allowed these artists to continue with their work despite the ridicule they received.

ACTIVITY 40: Tasting Crepes (Recipe)

Objectives: Exposure to multi-ethnic foods.

Ingredients:
- 2 eggs
- 1/4 teaspoon salt
- 2 tablespoons melted margarine
- 2/3 cup flour
- 1/3 cup milk
- a dash of sugar

Preparation: Beat the eggs. Add salt, sugar, and melted margarine. Next, add flour and milk. Beat. Cook in a crepe pan or hot oiled frying pan until bubbly. Then turn and cook until light brown. Use fresh fruit, vegetables, chocolate chips, or powdered (confectioners) sugar to roll up in the crepes.

Ask the Children: Does everyone in France eat crepes? (No.)

Tips: Other foods to taste may include omelets, croissants, and fruits grown in France, which the children may have already tasted (apples, peaches, cherries, oranges, raisins, and pears.) Cheese made from goat's and ewe's milk is more available in France than the cow's milk cheese we are used to in the United States. By the way, french fries, french dressing, and many other items in America called "french" were not originally French foods, although they can now be found in France as well as in many other countries.

ACTIVITY 41: Making Towers

Objectives: Creative design and construction, and fine-motor skills.

Preparation: Obtain a book from your library which contains a photograph of the Eiffel Tower. The Eiffel Tower is Paris' most prominent landmark, and was designed by a man named Gustav Eiffel. Now is a good time to mention the fact that the Statue of Liberty was made as a gift from France to the United States. It was brought to the United States in small pieces and then assembled.

Materials:
- Homemade Play Dough (*see recipe below)
- multi-colored pipe cleaners
- wooden sticks, such as frozen popsicle sticks
- a plastic lid for each child, such as a margarine lid
- glue, if requested

Procedure: Allow the children to play with the materials as they wish. They may place the play dough on the margarine lid and poke pipe cleaners and sticks into it to make a sculpture. The pipecleaners and sticks can be connected to one another or just poked into the clay.

---

* Recipe for Homemade Play Dough
(This recipe makes enough for four children.)

Objectives: Fine motor-skills, cause & effect, and creative expression.

- 2 1/2 cups flour
- 1 cup water
- 1 cup salt
- Food coloring if desired

Knead for approximately 10 minutes, or until you have reached the desired consistency. Dough sculpturing is an ancient tradition that is still practiced in France.

Tips: Before the activity, you could give each child a piece of paper and a pen, pencil, or marker and have them draw a design for a sculpture or tower.

UNIT FIVE
Amish American Cultural Aspects

UNIT FIVE: Amish American Cultural Aspects
Introduction

Amish (AH-mish) cultures exist in many parts of the United States. These religious groups are descendants of European immigrants. Each individual Amish community is unique unto itself, having varied languages, laws and cultural lifestyles. Amish people are generally found more in rural areas, while most Mennonite people are more urban and lead more liberal lifestyles. Some Mennonite people drive cars. While some Amish people accept rides in cars, horse-drawn carriages are their primary source of independent transportation.

In teaching children about other cultures, it is usually best to have a guest visitor of that particular culture. However, Amish people prefer to remain separate from other societies. Out of respect for their religiously motivated desire for privacy, please do not intrude by taking a field trip to see an Amish community. If you are located near an Amish community, you may wish to seek out a store that sells handmade Amish items such as quilts, dolls, furniture, or baked goods. You may also purchase handcrafts directly from designated craftspeople in certain Amish communities. For example, you may drive past a mailbox near the road with a sign that says, "Quilts," in which case you could purchase a quilt from that residence. It would be best to make this trip on your own, without your group of children.

Some of the objectives of this unit include: showing children that there are many unique cultures right within their own country; exposing children to and developing respect for lifestyles which differ from their own; examining the environmental benefits of using no electricity or cars; showing that the inner self of each person is what makes us special and likeable – not what we wear or what we own; giving children a sense of responsibility to care for and help their family, their community, and their world.

A beautiful book of photographs of Amish people is *Amish Odyssey* by Bill Coleman. Please see the Appendix for further information on this book.

UNIT FIVE: Amish American Cultural Aspects (Letter to Parents)

Date:

Dear Parents:

Our primary topic this week will be "Amish American Cultural Aspects." We will be learning that there are unique cultures right within our own country. Amish people of today dress much like European immigrants of 200 years ago.

A beautiful book of photographs of Amish people is *Amish Odyssey* by Bill Coleman, copyright 1988, published by St. James Press. An Amish cookbook you may wish to try is *Cooking from Quilt Country* by Marcia Adams, copyright 1989, published by Clarkson N. Potter, Inc.

We will be stressing self-esteem; each child is special for who he or she is, not for what he or she wears or owns. Through our activities, we will promote a sense of responsibility to care for and help our families, our community and our world. This also contributes to a children's sense of self-esteem and self-worth. We will encourage respect for different lifestyles which will include a "no electricity time."

You may wish to have a meal by candlelight to experience what it would be like to use no electricity. Environmentally speaking, candlelight is a great way to conserve energy. If you have any Amish handcrafts, we welcome you to come and show them to the children.

Sincerely,

ACTIVITY 42: Words from the German Language

Objectives: Appreciation for the use of other languages, linguistics and memory skills.

In many Amish communities English is spoken. In other areas, different languages are spoken such as German, Alsatian or a combination of several languages. Remember, languages vary greatly (both word usage and pronunciation) within themselves.

hallo (HAH low): *hello*

auf wiedersehen (owf VEE dah zay ehn): *goodbye*

mutti (MOO tee): *mom*

papa (PAH pah): *dad*

bubu (BUH buh): *another word for dad*

schatzi (SHUT zee): *sweetheart* - as said by an adult to a child
or **"schatz"** (shutz)

Wie gehts? (Vee GATES?): *How are you?*

ja (yah): *yes*

nein (nine): *no*

ACTIVITY 43: Pretend to Ride in a Horse-drawn Buggy

Objectives: Dramatic play, appreciation for cultural diversity.

Materials:
- a large cardboard box
- a blank audio cassette
- a tape recorder
- wooden blocks
- a jump rope

Preparation: Cut windows in the sides and back of the box. Color or paint the box black if desired. Record the clip-clop sound of wooden blocks, plastic bowls, or other items hitting a hard surface to simulate the sound of a horse's hooves on the pavement.

Procedure: Have the children climb aboard your pretend buggy. Turn on the tape recording of the simulated cadence of a horse's hooves hitting the pavement. If you have a rocking horse, the jump rope can be attached to it. The ends of the rope can be the reigns. The children can take turns going for buggy rides or even pretending to be the horse. You can use the simulated horse hooves tape to make up songs with or add rhythms to accompany the rhythm of the hooves. After this activity, allow the children to play freely with the box. Chances are, the buggy will "become" other things as the children use their imaginations to play creatively.

Tips: Many Amish people do accept rides in cars. Some get rides to their places of employment if they decide to work away from their farms. It will help the children to better understand what a horse-drawn buggy is if you also do an activity in which they can see a picture of a real one. Many parks in large cities offer horse-drawn carriage rides but they are generally very expensive.

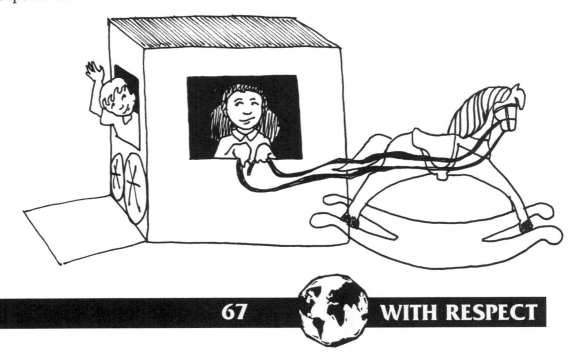

ACTIVITY 44: A Horse-drawn Buggy Toy

Objectives: Dramatic play, creative expression.

Materials:
- a large tissue box
- black acrylic paint
- two unsharpened pencils
- two 8-oz. size margarine lids
- two 16-oz. size cottage cheese lids

For the teacher:
- sharp scissors
- a permanent black marker
- two 12" pieces of yarn
- tape or a stapler
- a small orange paper triangle
- a toy horse or photocopy of a horse illustration

Procedure: Cut the tissue box as shown. Use the scissors or a hole puncher to poke holes in the center of each lid, and poke holes in the box as shown. Insert the pencils through the lids and holes in the box to attach the wheels. Tape or staple the yarn to the front of the box (carriage) as reigns. The other end of the reigns can be attached to a toy horse. The buggy can be painted black. An orange paper triangle (slow-moving vehicle sign) can be attached to the back of the buggy. Use the permanent marker to draw spokes on the wheels.

Tips: One buggy can be made by the teacher and shared among the children. If your group of children is at a developmental level in which they are capable of doing most of these steps themselves, then the children may wish to make their own.

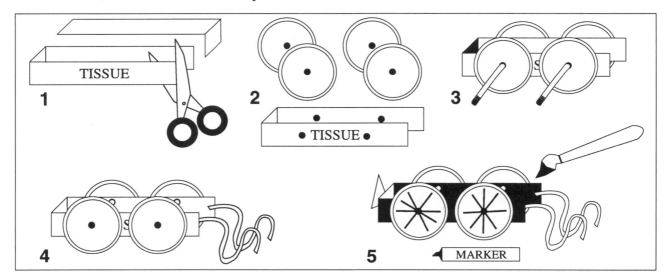

ACTIVITY 45: Cars vs. Buggies

Objectives: Science, environmental awareness, observation skills.

Preparation: Take the children outside to watch traffic on the road outside your school, or record the sounds of a busy intersection on the other side of the tape from Activity 42. You may wish to obtain a toy car or plastic truck to use with your horse-drawn buggy toy.

Procedure: Ask the children to list differences and similarities between cars and buggies. For example, "If you wanted to go somewhere, which one would you use?" (Both.) Use this opportunity to discuss the effects of noise pollution and air pollution on our environment.

Ask the Children: What is air pollution? Which makes our air dirtier – cars or buggies? How does pollution hurt living things? Which moves faster, cars or horses and buggies? Which is noisier, cars or buggies?

WITH RESPECT

ACTIVITY 46: Amish Brown Sugar Pie (Recipe)

Objective: Exposure to multi-ethnic foods.

This is an old recipe which has been passed on through generations of Amish people and is now published in a cookbook. It is important for the children to know that Amish people today include foods similar to what the children eat in their diets. I know several Amish families that eat foods such as hot dogs, soda, sugar-coated breakfast cereals, and other foods which can be purchased at their local grocery stores. Also included within the meals of many families are foods which have been home-grown, home-canned, and often hunted for. Foods eaten vary from community to community and can go along with the language spoken there; i.e. German foods and German language are present in Elkhart and La Grange counties in Indiana.

Sugar milk pies were called "miliche flitche," or "poor man's pie," because of the simplicity of their ingredients. People beg for this recipe, for it is what they remember eating as a child, but can never find in cookbooks. These are the kinds of recipes that are in danger of becoming lost. This is the reason why this cookbook came into being. Don't be afraid to mix the pie right in the shell, it is a good way to save time.

Ingredients:
- 1 unbaked 8-inch pie shell
- 1 cup brown sugar
- 2 1/2 tablespoons butter
- 1 12-oz. can of evaporated milk
- 3 tablespoons all-purpose flour
- ground cinnamon
- speck of salt

Procedure: Preheat oven to 350 degrees. Place the brown sugar, flour and salt in the pie shell and mix with your fingers. Pour the evaporated milk over the flour and sugar, but do not stir or mix this in. Dot with butter, and drift cinnamon liberally over all. Bake for 50 minutes or until the filling just bubbles up in the middle.

The filling will never completely set, but that's the way it's supposed to be. This pie is better eaten at room temperature. If you refrigerate leftovers (it is highly unlikely there will be leftovers), reheat them in the oven before serving.

Tips: Recipe can be doubled and prepared in a 10-inch pie shell. For that size, bake 1 hour and 20 minutes. This recipe and its accompanying information are reprinted with permission from *Cooking from Quilt Country* by Marcia Adams. Please see the Appendix for more information on this book.

ACTIVITY 47: A Cooperative Quilt

Objectives: Fine-motor skills, creative expression, and small group cooperative skills.

Materials:
- two similar-sized squares cut from tissue or cereal boxes for each child
- a hole punch
- yarn
- a real hand-stitched quilt for the children to see

Preparation: After you have cut two squares of the desired material for each child, punch a hole in the corner of each square. Next, cut several strands of yarn so the children can connect the squares.

Procedure: Have the children use yarn (with one end knotted and the other end wrapped in tape) to lace their two squares together. Then they can cooperatively sew all of their squares together. If your group size is quite large, you may wish to separate into small groups. The children may wish to color, paint, or glue on fabric or felt pieces to decorate their quilt(s).

Tips: You might ask parents or fellow teachers to contribute unwanted clothing to cut cloth squares for your quilt. Quilts are often made cooperatively by Amish women. One Amish woman I know completes one quilt each week with the help of her four daughters. It would take her much more time if she were to make quilts alone. Full-size quilts sell for several hundred dollars. Considering the expense of materials and the time involved, it's a reasonable price for a work of art such as a quilt. Quilting is an age-old and important part of many different cultures in many parts of the world.

WITH RESPECT

Quilt Patterns

ACTIVITY 48: Black Out

Objectives: Appreciation for cultural diversity, observation skills, and energy awareness.

Materials:
- many candles and lanterns
- a childproof lighter or book of matches

Fire Safety Note: The matches, candles, and lanterns must be carefully placed out of the children's reach. No balls or other "throwing toys" should be used during this time. Story, snack, and meal times are ideal for using no electricity because the children's activity level is low.

Procedure: Have a snack, story or meal by candlelight. Restate your fire safety rules about things that are hot and "untouchable."

Ask the Children: If I wanted to cook something and I didn't use a modern stove, how could I do it? (Wood-burning stove.) If I wanted music and didn't use electricity, what could I do? (Sing.) If I didn't have a telephone, but I wanted to talk to a neighbor, what could I do? (Visit or send a letter.) What are some things in the classroom that use electricity?

Tips: Most Amish people do sing. In fact, many teenagers gather together for evening sing-a-longs. However, most do not use musical instruments.

WITH RESPECT

ACTIVITY 49: Amish Song or Poem

Objectives: Cultural diversity and similarity, music and rhythm skills.

I Am Amish

Refrain:
My mother is Amish.
My father's Amish too.
And I am Amish,
But I'm a lot like you.

Verses:
Oh, there are things we do that are different too.
We don't drive cars or trucks.
I ride in a buggy with a horse in the front,
and it takes me to my school.
(To refrain)

Oh, there are things we do that are different too.
We don't use electric lights.
We use special lanterns and candles too,
and they light up my home.
(To refrain)

Oh, there are things we do just the same as you.
I work and help at home.
I play and I laugh, and I eat and sleep,
and I love my family.
(To refrain)

Tips: This song can be found on the audio cassette, *Music With Respect, Volume 1-2P.* Please see the Appendix for details.

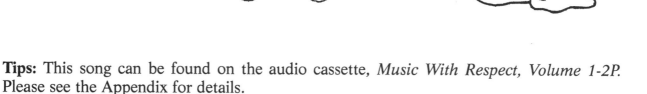

ACTIVITY 50: Barn Raising – Cooperative Community Efforts

Objectives: Cooperative social skills, gross-motor skills.

Materials:
- tape in a dispenser or masking tape
- scissors
- paper grocery bags
- a large empty wall

Preparation: You may want to make a barn-shaped outline on the wall in masking tape so the children know where to start "building."

Procedure: Ask the children to pretend that their neighbor's barn has burned down and that they have all come together to help build a new barn. They can cut their paper bags into strips or pieces as they wish. Then they can tape the pieces on the wall to represent pieces of the barn. The barn can be painted afterwards if desired.

Ask the Children: Do only Amish people build barns? What do people keep in barns? Are there any barns around here?

Tips: A few years ago in Pennsylvania, 12 barns belonging to Amish people were burned to the ground by an arsonist(s). When there is a disaster such as this within their own community as well as outside their community, Amish people donate generous gifts of work and time to help others. The barns in Pennsylvania were rebuilt so quickly, it was a disadvantage to police attempting to investigate the crime. Children can understand how good it feels to help someone else. They can already begin to feel secure in being an important part of a community effort.

ACTIVITY 51: Rag Baby Doll

Objectives: Craft making, fine-motor skills, cultural diversity.

Materials:
- an old sock from home
- rags or old clothes for stuffing
- yarn
- coffee filters cut in half (one half per child)
- a hole punch
- scissors

Preparation: To make bonnets for the dolls, punch a hole in the two corners of each coffee filter half. Tie a piece of yarn through each hole to make ties.

Procedure: Allow each child to make a baby doll with the sock they have brought from home. Have them stuff the sock with rags. Then give each child a piece of yarn which can be wrapped around to form the doll's neck. Other rags may be used as blankets for their dolls. Legs can be made by making a single cut through both layers in the open end of the sock. You can help the children with tying the legs together to hold the stuffing in. Explain to the children that some Amish children play with dolls similar to the dolls that other children play with. However, many Amish children play with faceless homemade dolls. Give the children the option of leaving their dolls faceless, or gluing on small scraps of cloth to make a face.

Tips: Most Amish communities allow their children to play only with handmade faceless dolls since the use of graven images is against their religious beliefs. However, there are now some communities which do allow the use of contemporary plastic baby dolls.

UNIT SIX
Touch

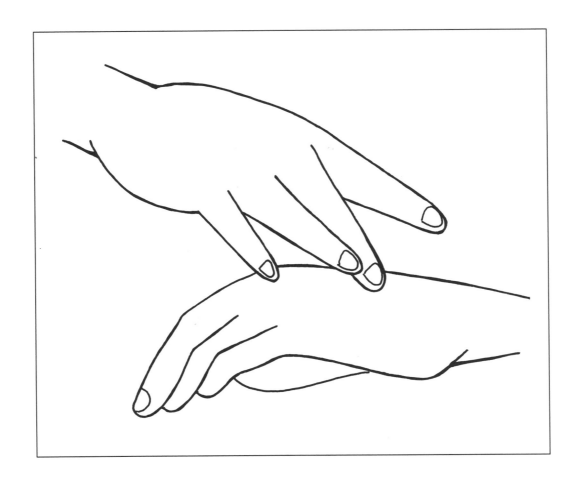

UNIT SIX: Touch
Introduction

Learning through touching, exploring, and doing enhances a child's natural curiosity. Whenever possible, allow the children to explore new things by not only seeing, but by touching. The sensory activities in this unit can help expand the children's vocabularies as they find words to describe the textures they are feeling. By engaging all of the senses in any activity, you are giving the children a well-rounded educational experience that they are more likely to learn from and retain.

There are several possibilities for tangent topics to use within this unit. One extremely sensitive but important topic is the prevention of sexual abuse. Be certain to send a note home with each child to be signed by parents giving you permission to discuss this topic. Please see the proposed parent letter in this section as an example. Explain to the parents how very simply it will be discussed.

Here are a few examples of some short but powerful phrases to use with the children: There are good touches and bad touches; If someone touches you by hugging, kissing or tickling, it can be a very good touch; If someone touches or wants to see your private parts, it is bad; Private parts are the parts of your body that your underpants cover up; If someone ever tries to give you a bad touch, yell, 'No!' then run away and tell someone; The only people who can check your private parts are your doctor and your parents. This is to make sure you're healthy.

UNIT SIX: Touch (Letter to Parents)

Date:

Dear Parents:

This week our primary unit is the "Sense of Touch." We will be playing sensory games which will help the children become more aware of how much we use and rely upon our sense of touch. Touch plays a vital role in a child's early learning experiences. Here's an example of how bland learning can be without sensory exploration: A four year old boy had been learning about snakes. After a week of snake books, snake songs, snake art projects, and colorful photographs of snakes, the boy commented, "But snakes aren't real." This example shows that for young children's learning experiences, real-life sensory exploration is most effective.

Another aspect we will be including in this unit will be protective behavior. This includes the understanding that everyone has the right to feel safe, and how to prevent becoming a victim of sexual abuse. This topic will not be discussed in great depth. The object is to give the children the idea that their body is their own and no one has the right to see or touch private parts except the child's parents and physician to be sure the child is healthy.

Please fill in the permission form at the bottom of the page if your child may be present during discussion of this topic, and return it tomorrow.

Sincerely,

_____ may OR may not (circle one)
(Child's Name)

participate in the discussion on protective behavior at

_____ on _____
(Day Care or School)   (Date)

_____   _____
(Parent Signature)   (Date)

Please feel free to discuss this important topic with your child. If you have any questions or comments, please send a note.

ACTIVITY 52: Texture Board

Objectives: Introduction to different textures, tactile and visual discrimination.

Suggested Textures Include:
- *bumpy:* corrugated cardboard
- *rough:* sandpaper
- *smooth:* foil or satin ribbons
- *soft:* fabric scraps such as flannel or velvet
- *prickly:* small clippings of coarse outdoor rug or steel wool
- *cushy:* pieces of a sponge

Use your imagination and you'll be amazed at what different types of textures you can find to introduce to the children.

Preparation: Gather several different materials for this activity. You might want to just use objects found in the classroom for ease, but a lot of variety works the best. Either prepare your texture board with or without the help of the children.

Procedure: Once your texture board is complete, point to the different materials and ask the children how they'd expect them to feel. Then, one by one, let them come and touch the board.

Ask the Children: What are some other smooth objects? What are some rough objects?

Tips: Suggestions for simplifying cleanup after messy art projects, which are perfect for this unit, include:
- line the table and floor with newspaper
- use inexpensive plastic, vinyl or homemade contact paper placemats for using clay or Play Dough. (See Activity 41 for this recipe.)

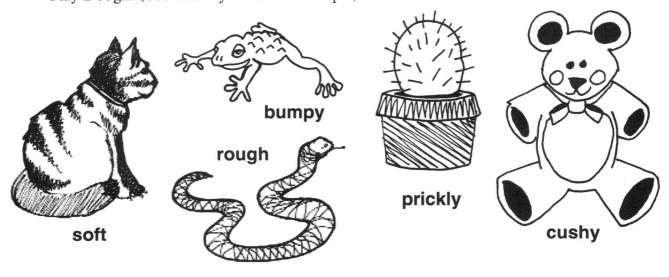

soft   rough   bumpy   prickly   cushy

ACTIVITY 53: Aquarium Gravel Collages

Objectives: Tactile exploration, fine-motor skills, and creative expression.

Materials:
- colored aquarium gravel (rinsed and dried)
- heavy paper
- glue

Procedure: Have the children drizzle glue across their papers. Then have them cover the glue with aquarium gravel, and tip one end of their papers up to remove the loose gravel. The idea here isn't to make a picture, just to create a rough texture. If you have the time, you could write each child's name in glue for them and then have them apply the stones.

Tips: You might want to let the children make several layers of gravel for more texture, but this takes a longer time to dry. Keep these collages, or some of your own, to use later on in the unit as a comparison to other textures.

ACTIVITY 54: Identifying Nature Items Through Sense of Touch

Objectives: Memory, sensory, and observation skills.

Preparation: Take the children on a nature walk. Have them each bring along a paper lunch bag for collecting things. Items to be collected can include small pine cones, pebbles, feathers, acorn shells or other nut shells, dried grasses or weeds, small twigs, leaves, and dead pine branches. Tell the children to only collect things found on the ground – no living plants or insects! Instruct the children that pulling live plants from the ground can kill them.

Procedure: Have the children reach into their bags to hold an object and feel it while leaving it in the bag and out of their sight. Ask them what they think that they are touching. Have them identify the objects one at a time by feeling them, and then removing them from the bag to see if their guesses are correct. This is a wonderful memory game as well as a sensory activity.

Tips: Save these items for the next activity.

ACTIVITY 55: Nature Textures Collage

Objectives: Science, visual and tactile exploration, creative expression, and gross-motor skills.

Materials:
- items collected on the nature walk of the previous activity
- heavy paper
- glue

Procedure: Distribute an assortment of the listed materials to each child on a tray or paper plate. Then the children can choose the items they want, using glue to attach the objects collected from the nature walk onto heavy paper, making a beautiful collage. You could also have children make theme collages, using all wood items, or leaves only. Other backgrounds can be used such as styrofoam trays, poster board, shoe box lids (contact a shoe store for empty boxes), cardboard, or paper plates.

If a nature walk is not possible to take with your group of children, you may wish to have the children construct different kinds of collages. A scraps collage also uses a child's tactile and creative skills. The following is a list of further materials you might like to use.

Suggested Ideas for Materials:
- Buttons
- Fabric scraps
- Small beads
- Small pieces of pipe cleaners (these can be pre-cut with metal scissors)
- Cut-up paper doilies
- Yarn
- Scraps of ribbons, cut-up used bows from gifts
- Cotton balls
- Cut-up plastic net-type produce bags
- Tongue depressors or frozen pop sticks
- Milk lids

Tips: Collages provide lots of artistic freedom for little hands. Children will feel good about their abilities when they take scraps and pieces of junk to make a beautiful piece of art. This is another project you might want to display in your library or in your classroom.

ACTIVITY 56: Prickly Porcupines

Objectives: Tactile and visual exploration, cause & effect, and creative expression.

Materials for each child:
- Homemade Play Dough (see Activity 41 for recipe)
- colored toothpicks (preferably the round type)
- buttons
- dark colored pebbles

Procedure: Divide the play dough among the children. Allow plenty of free play time with the play dough. Then show them how to form an egg shape to begin making their porcupines. Pass out dark colored buttons (eyes) and dark colored pebbles (noses) to each child to make faces on their porcupines. Next, pass out toothpicks to each child. The children can poke the toothpicks into their porcupines to make quills. Baking racks work well for drying. If the children wish to take their porcupines home that day, you can place each porcupine on a small paper plate. Suggest that the porcupines be dried on a wire baking rack at home in order for the bottoms to be exposed to air.

Ask the Children: Why do you think the porcupine is prickly? Do you know of any other things which are prickly?

Tips: Making a porcupine "correctly" is not necessary. Perhaps a child will make something different, such as a cactus, or simply enjoy the experience of poking items into play dough. The process of learning is what is important, not the end result. You may wish to do this activity during units on the letter "P" for porcupine, or "Q" for quill.

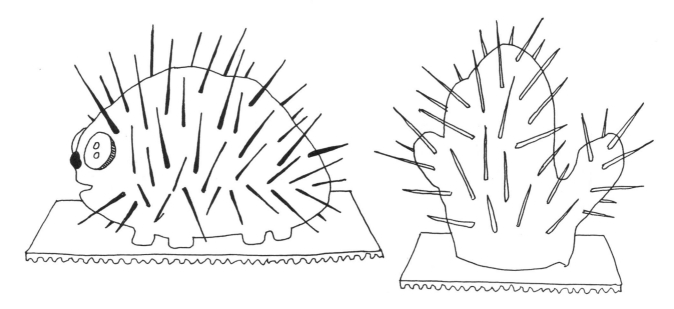

ACTIVITY 57: Touching With Covered Hands

Objectives: Tactile exploration and cognitive skills.

Materials:
- gloves or mittens (one per child)
- different objects and textures to feel
- *optional:* eye covers (see directions for making these below)

Procedure: Have the children wear eye covers or tell them to close their eyes. Next, have them each put on one glove or mitten, and pass them different objects and textures to feel and identify if they can. After feeling each object, the children can remove their gloves or mittens and feel it again. If they still have trouble identifying the object, give them hints and clues before you let them use their eyes.

Ask the Children: Which way was easier to identify the objects – with or without the gloves? How would you be able to feel if you did not have arms or hands? (With your feet, toes and face.)

Making Eye Covers

These can be made by the teacher. For health purposes, make one per child, label them with each child's name, and do not allow the children to share them. Collect the eye covers after use in order to use them again in future activities within the units on senses.

Materials:
- black construction paper
- yarn
- scissors
- a hole punch
- white crayon or chalk for drawing pattern and labeling

Instructions: Cut black construction paper into rectangles (approximately 2" x 5 1/2".) Cut out a small triangular notch for the nose. Punch a hole at each end of the rectangles. Thread an 18" piece of yarn into each hole and tie a knot. The finished eye covers can be tied onto the children and will resemble sunglasses in appearance.

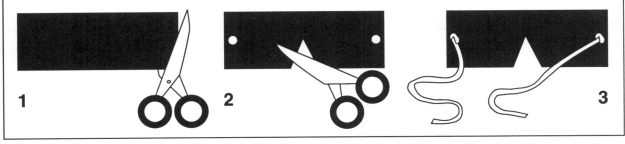

ACTIVITY 58: Snack Suggestion – Finger Gelatin

Objectives: Tactile stimulation, creative expression, and fine-motor skills.

Procedure: Fruit flavored finger gelatin may be made using fruit juice in place of water. The recipe is on the package. You may wish to make the gelatin in a 9"x12" cake pan. Cut each child a square of gelatin. Give them small cookie cutters and plastic knives to use before they eat so that they can try and make shapes, animals, or simply play with the gelatin's unique texture.

Tips: Make sure all of the children wash their hands thoroughly both before and after this activity.

ACTIVITY 59: Now You Can Play With Your Food (and eat it too!)

Objectives: Fine-motor and manipulation skills, and nutrition.

Materials:
- prepared mashed potatoes (instant ones work very well, make about one third of a cup for each child)
- heavy duty zip seal bags (one per child)
- grated parmesan or cheddar cheese
- margarine
- plates
- spoons

Preparation: Prepare the mashed potatoes and place approximately one third of a cup of potatoes into each of the zip seal bags. When the potatoes are warm, not hot, have the children wash their hands and come to the table. Give each child a sealed bag of potatoes, and announce, "Kids, you aren't usually allowed to play with your food, but right now you may!" Instruct them not to open the sealed bags.

Procedure: Allow the children to poke, squeeze, and manipulate the potatoes within the bags. It's a truly unusual sensory experience which children love doing. After the children have had plenty of time with the unopened bags of potatoes, you can offer them a spoon and let them open their bags to eat their potatoes. The potatoes can be eaten right out of the bags, or placed on plates, and topped with margarine and grated cheese.

ACTIVITY 60: Identifying Variance in Sense of Touch

Objectives: Protective behavior and sensory exploration.

Materials:
- feathers (one for each group of two children)
- *optional:* eye covers (see Activity 57 for how to make these)

Procedure: Have the children find a partner. Offer to be the partner of a child if one is left out. Have one child in each group wear eye covers or close their eyes. The other child will then tickle that child with a feather. The child with the eye covers must tell where they felt the tickle. Then have the children switch places with their partners.

Ask the Children: Which places were most ticklish?

Tips: Now is an opportune time to discuss with the children the following: it is never acceptable to touch someone else's private parts; it is never acceptable to allow someone else to touch or see their private parts. Ask the children, "What should you do if someone does this?" (Yell, "NO!" and tell a different adult.) The exception is a parent or doctor who is trying to clean them or check them for physical wellness. Send home the note to inform parents that you will be discussing protective behavior and receive their permissions prior to this activity.

WITH RESPECT

ACTIVITY 61: Secret Socks

Objectives: Social skills and tactile exploration.

Materials:
- a large sock (one for every two children)
- several small items to fit inside of the socks

Procedure: Have each child find a partner. One of the partners can leave the room with a sock and fill it with several objects. After he returns his partner can reach his hand into the sock to identify the objects only by touching them inside the sock.

Tips: You might want to give hints to the children on hard to identify objects. Ask the children to use the words to describe the textures they feel, for texture vocabulary usage.

ACTIVITY 62: Texture Books

Objectives: Language/vocabulary, tactile exploration, and fostering a love of books.

Materials:
- index cards
- scraps of textured materials (such as cotton balls, packing peanuts, corrugated cardboard, sandpaper, and foil)
- fabric scraps (such as satin, flannel, velvet, or corduroy)
- glue
- a hole punch
- yarn

Procedure: Have the children glue each different texture onto a separate index card to make pages for their books. After the pages have dried, put each book together, and hole punch and bind them with yarn. Have the children describe with words how the different textures feel.

ACTIVITY 63: Bookmaking

Objectives: Visual and tactile skills, fine-motor skills, and fostering a love of books.

Materials:
- a hole punch
- yarn
- scraps of paper, cardboard, and material for pages

Preparation: Book making can help a child's love for books grow tremendously. Remember the first time you made something for yourself and how wonderful it was because it was made exactly as you liked it? Similar feelings can be aroused within a child; the enjoyment and pride in "reading" (at a pre-reading level) a book that a child has made by himself and about himself can be wonderful. Children can even do the binding themselves with your close supervision. Staplers work well for books that are not too thick. Hole punchers and metal paper fasteners are fun for children to use as well. Offer the children different choices and sizes of materials for book pages. Small paper plates, cardboard pieces, foil, and fabric squares are a few examples of interesting book page materials.

Procedure: Offer the children as many shapes and types of similarly-sized scraps as possible to choose as pages for their own personal "books." Allow them creative freedom to draw on some of the pages, or crinkle them up, glue other items on the pages, etc. If your children are at an appropriate age level, ask them to "read" their books to you, using their powerful imagination and ingenuity.

ACTIVITY 64: "Touch or Don't Touch" Game

Objectives: Safety, whole language/reading skills.

Materials:
- items unsafe to touch (a coffee mug, a sharp knife, any small appliance with an electrical cord, a curling iron, a toaster, a pan, etc.)
- items which are safe to touch (various toys, food given by a trusted adult, clothes, books, etc.)
- a piece of paper with the word, "Touch"
- a piece of paper that says, "Don't touch"

Procedure: Hold up each item and ask the children what it is. Then ask them if they should touch it or not, and then have them place it near the "Touch" or "Don't touch" sign.

Ask the Children: Can you name some more items that are unsafe to touch? Do you know why they are unsafe?

Tips: This exercise will be most effective if you offer the children explanations for not touching certain items. Explain why each object is dangerous so they understand the rule.

UNIT SEVEN
Taste

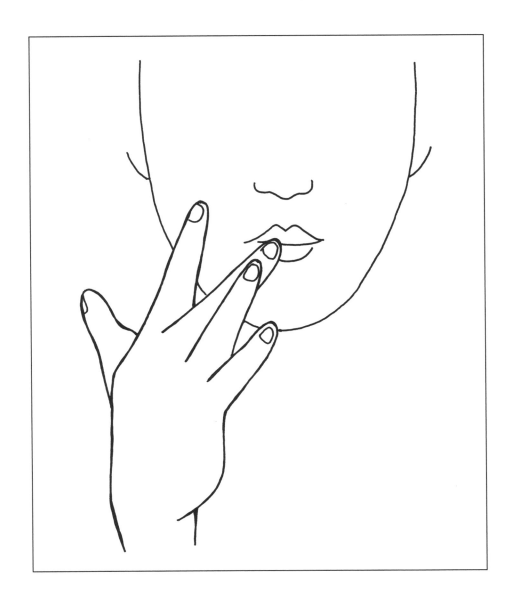

UNIT SEVEN: Taste
Introduction

Children's food preferences change frequently. They may taste an unusually sour piece of fruit which curbs their enthusiasm to eat it ever again. Perhaps they'll taste a familiar food which was prepared differently from the way it's done at home (i.e. different seasonings, cooking methods or time lengths, and temperature when served) and not to the child's liking. The child may then refuse to eat that food altogether. Therefore, it's important to keep offering foods without insisting that they be tasted, even if they were previously disliked by a child. If a child does not want a certain food, please respect his or her wishes. We must also respect cultural influences on food preferences of young children. A friend and colleague of mine once told me of a child new to her day care from Poland. The child did not speak English and was upset at lunch time every day. After help from a language interpreter, it was discovered that the child was very upset to have to drink his milk cold. The child's milk was warmed for him daily from then on. The other children also became interested in trying their milk warm which helped them to respect another's individual preferences. If children are not forced to try new foods, nor to clean their plates, they will be more willing to try new foods. This is important information that should be shared with parents, since the attitudes towards eating learned in a child's home will prevail during the meals eaten away from home.

It is also important to teach children that only the food and drink they get from families, caregivers, and schools should be accepted. Candy found on the ground should never be tasted, since candy and harmful drugs often look remarkably similar. A puppet show such as the one suggested in this unit's activity section can be an effective method of sending this important message to children. Considering the great number of children who explore things by mouthing them, this is a wise reminder for children even at the elementary school level.

UNIT SEVEN: Taste (Letter to Parents)

Date:

Dear Parents:

This week our primary topic is the "Sense of Taste." Some of our activities will include: flavor tasting games, tasting new foods, and a puppet show that will teach the children about the dangers of drinking or eating anything they may find that looks like food or candy. Potentially harmful medications and candy often look remarkably similar.

At Home Ideas: Ask your child what he or she would do if a stranger offered candy, gum, money, or presents. Discuss the "Say, 'No!'" rule. Also ask your child if it is okay to eat food which he or she finds on the floor or outside on the ground. Ask, "Why isn't it okay?"

Since children's food preferences change frequently, foods previously disliked should not be cut out of your menu entirely. Tasting a fruit that was especially sour or a food that burned their tongue is enough to cause a child to refuse a certain food for a while. Offering a child food does not mean putting it on his or her plate, it means to ask if the child would like any. After watching others enjoy foods that the child had disliked previously, chances are excellent that he or she will ask to taste that food once again at some point. They may ask for a very small portion, which is the best idea anyway. That way, there won't be any wasted if they don't like it, or they can simply ask for more. Psychologists now know that many eating disorders are linked to a person's childhood eating experiences. For example, a child who is rewarded with food and treats may associate them with being loved. As an adult obesity may occur as the person binges on sweets to attempt to rekindle those childhood feelings of love. Pediatric experts now recommend that food be neither given as a reward, nor withheld as a punishment. Many parents encourage their children to overeat by insisting that they clean their plates, or give great praise when they do. Wasting food is undoubtedly not good. Serving a child very small portions can help prevent this problem. A relaxed atmosphere in which a child is neither forced to eat new foods nor to clean their plate is best for a child. Then he or she can feel good about making the choice to taste new foods and liking them.

Our rules here are based upon one basic principal, "No hurting allowed," which includes people's feelings. Therefore, statements such as, "Yuch!!" "I hate this!!" "How can you eat that?! You're gross!!" are not acceptable. A simple, "No thank you" if a child doesn't want a particular food is preferable. Respecting differences in people's food (or other) preferences is an important concept for children to learn. Also, the person who worked very hard to prepare food may hear the child say, "Yuch!" and feel bad. Giving the children reasons for rules makes them more willing and able to follow them.

Sincerely,

 **WITH RESPECT**

ACTIVITY 65: Taste Tests

Objectives: Distinguishing flavors, sensory skills.

Materials:
- four popsicle sticks for each child
- four plastic containers, such as margarine tubs
- salt
- lemon juice
- honey or sugar
- instant decaffeinated coffee

Preparation: Put the salt, lemon juice, honey or sugar, and instant coffee in separate containers. Place the popsicle sticks (which will be used for tasting) into half of a glass of water, leaving one end dry. Then dip each stick into a different flavor and the granulated foods will adhere to the moistened sticks. Prepare one stick with each of the four flavors for each child.

Procedure: Have the children taste the four different flavors on their sticks and try to identify which one is sweet, sour, salty, or bitter. (Do the bitter one - coffee, last.) Make sure to have juice, water, or milk ready if the children request it after this activity.

Tips: See following activity for an extended and more advanced version of this game.

ACTIVITY 66: Discovering Our Taste Buds

Objectives: Science, taste discrimination, observation skills.

Materials:
- hand mirrors (one per child or small group of children)
- materials used in the previous activity

Procedure: Give each child a hand mirror and the same taste test materials as the previous activity. First have them look at their tongues to visualize their taste buds. Next have them place a flavor onto various places on their tongues to locate where the different types of taste buds are located.

Ask the Children: Where are your sweet taste buds? Where are your bitter, salty, and sour taste buds? What other words could you use to describe these tastes?

Tips: The taste buds are located from back to front in the following order: bitter, sour, salty, and sweet. So, the children can experiment with putting sugar or honey on the tip of their tongues, or lemon juice in the back of the tongue, etc.

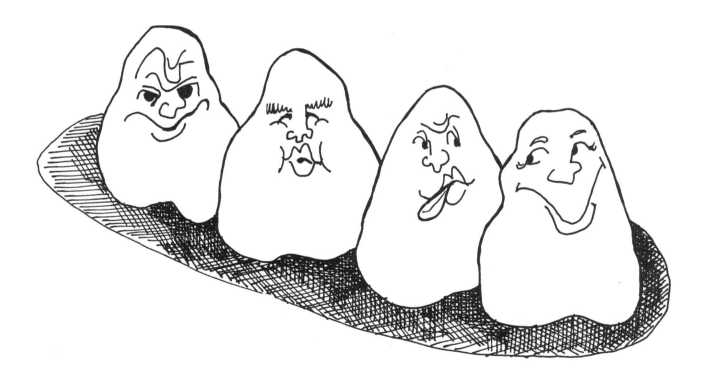

ACTIVITY 67: "My Favorite Foods" Book

Objectives: Self-concept, nutrition, fine-motor and writing skills.

Materials:
- old magazines with pictures of food (make certain to include ethnically diverse examples)
- halved sheets of construction paper or large unlined index cards
- glue
- a hole punch
- yarn
- markers

Procedure: Have the children cut or tear out pictures of foods they like from the magazines. If some of their favorite foods are not pictured in a magazine, encourage the children to draw pictures of those foods. Have them glue or draw the pictures onto either halved pieces of construction paper or index cards for their book pages.

Have the children decorate the cover pages of their books however they would like, and write their names on them. For the children who can't write their names, hold their hands while you guide them to write their name saying or singing each letter aloud as you write it. For example, each letter of the name, "David" could be sung to the tune of "E-I-E-I-O." Other names will fit well to the tune of "Twinkle, Twinkle, Little Star." After you have helped them write their names, you may wish to "dot-to-dot" write their names for them, and have them connect the dots having almost printed their names themselves. After having done these two steps with the children a few times, they will begin experimenting with printing letters in their names on their own. The letters will be in random order, backwards, and varied in sizes, which is absolutely normal.

Ask the Children: What their favorite foods are and point out the vast variety of food preferences. (i.e., I like broccoli and Antonio doesn't. Antonio, do you like me even if I like a food that you don't like?) Do we all have to like the same foods, toys, games or music in order to like each other?

Tips: If the children do not object to your writing in their books, ask them what they'd like you to write on each page. This helps the children's visual awareness of print. Allow the children to "read" their books to each other at story time.

ACTIVITY 68: Feet That Can Taste

Objectives: Science and observation skills.

Materials:
- a butterfly net
- a clear plastic container, such as a peanut butter jar
- netting or paper towel with holes punched in it for air

Preparation: Use a butterfly net to capture a housefly. Place it in the container with holes in the top for air.

Procedure: Observe the fly inside the clear, plastic container. It rubs it's front feet together frequently to clean them. Even though it has a separate mouth for eating, it smells tastes with its feet. Butterflies and many arachnids such as tarantulas also taste with their front feet.

Ask the Children: Can you tell how something is going to taste just by seeing it? What about smelling it?

Tips: You may want to bring a magnifying glass for the children to help them watch the fly's tiny movements. Placing a small piece of bread or a drop of juice in the container will help you observe this phenomena, if the fly is not "tasting" anything.

ACTIVITY 69: Puppets That Can Eat

Objectives: Arts and crafts, nutrition, dramatic play, and fine-motor coordination.

Materials for each child:
- a paper lunch bag
- markers
- scissors
- construction paper
- glue
- yarn (for hair)
- fabric scraps (for clothing)

Procedure: Have each child poke a hole into their own paper bag with a marker or scissors in the crease in the folded flap of the bag to make a mouth large enough in which to put pretend food.

Next have the children design their own puppet people using the materials suggested along with any others you may have on hand, such as buttons for eyes or clothing.

For making pretend food for your puppets, have the children make food out of either Homemade Play Dough (See Activity 41) or construction paper. Have the children make small foods such as carrots, apples, slices of pizza, or any other favorite treat. These foods should be small enough to fit into their puppets' mouths.

Tips: If your children are not at an age where they can construct their own puppets, have them make their favorite foods out of the dough and take turns feeding a puppet that you make.

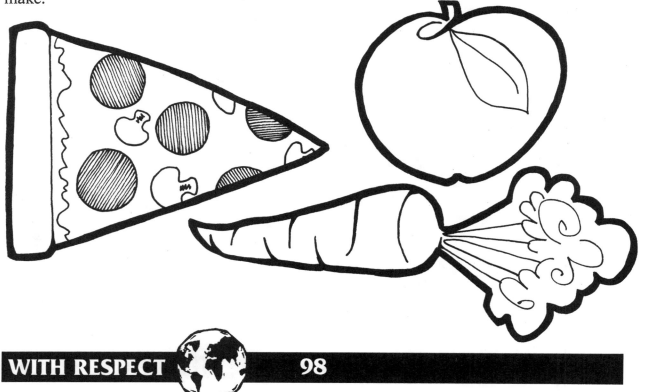

WITH RESPECT

ACTIVITY 70: Danger! - Never Eat Foods You Find! (Puppet Show)

Objectives: Safety, dramatic play.

Materials:
- a puppet made in the previous activity
- several colorful pieces of candy which look similar to medicine
- a father or mother puppet
- *optional:* a shoe box to simulate an ambulance

Puppet Show: The puppet finds something on the sidewalk that he thinks is candy. He eats it but becomes very sick. The puppet is taken to the hospital in an ambulance. After the puppet wakes up in the hospital and feels better, he tells his parent that he ate something he found which looked like candy. His parent tells him that it was not candy, but serious medicine which made him very sick. The puppet tells his parent that he will never again eat something he finds.

Ask the Children: If you find something that looks like candy, what should you do? If an adult that you don't know, or a child that you don't know offers you food or drink, what should you do? (Say "NO!" or ask a trusted adult.)

Tips: Show the children several colorful pieces of candy that look similar to medicine. Tell them that if they find something that looks like candy, they should not eat it!

ACTIVITY 71: The Official Food Taster (Puppet Show)

Objectives: Nutrition, dramatic play.

Materials:
- a puppet and pretend food for it to eat (see Activity 69)
- another family member puppet (possibly a grandparent, mother, or father). This is an opportune time to remind the children that not every family means "a child living with a mother and a father."

Puppet Show: The puppet refuses to taste new foods that are offered by his family. One day the puppet decides to taste a new food, and loves it! From then on, he decides he will be the family's "Official New Food Taster."

Ask the Children: Do you have any foods that you love/hate? Have you ever tried and liked a food you thought you wouldn't like?

Tips: Reinforce the idea that children should only eat or drink that which is given to them by a trusted adult. Encourage children to try new things, or ask their families for new foods to try from other countries and other cultures.

ACTIVITY 72: Food Tasting Parties

Objectives: Nutrition, social skills, respecting individual preferences.

Materials:
- several types of fruits, vegetables, breads, and cheeses

Preparation: Designate four days of a week to be "food tasting party days," such as Tuesday: fruit tasting party, Wednesday: vegetable tasting party, etc. If the cost of buying so many varied food items is too high for your budget, send a note home with each parent requesting that they each bring in a different type of fruit, cheese, etc.

One important goal within this activity is to allow the children to see how varied our individual preferences are. Helping them to understand and respect the unique tastes which we all have can help them to accept each person exactly as they are.

Whole Language Extended Activity: Charts can be posted with each child's name down the side, and different foods along the top column. To signify if a child likes a new food, write, "Yes" on the chart. If the child dislikes a certain food write, "No" on the chart and if the child chooses not to taste or try a certain food, put a question mark in the space. The children can learn to recognize the words, "YES," and "NO," their friends' names, and the question mark symbol. You can ask the children questions such as, "Does Juan like broccoli?" and point to the answer on the chart as they answer together aloud.

Ask the Children: If I like broccoli and Vanessa does not, can we still like each other?

Tips: Never force or pressure a child into trying a new food. Also, you might want to ask children if they like foods one by one in varying order. Sometimes, if everyone else hates a food, and one child likes it, they'll feel pressured into saying they hate the food, too. Encourage the children to be honest in their opinions, even if they are different.

UNIT EIGHT
Hearing

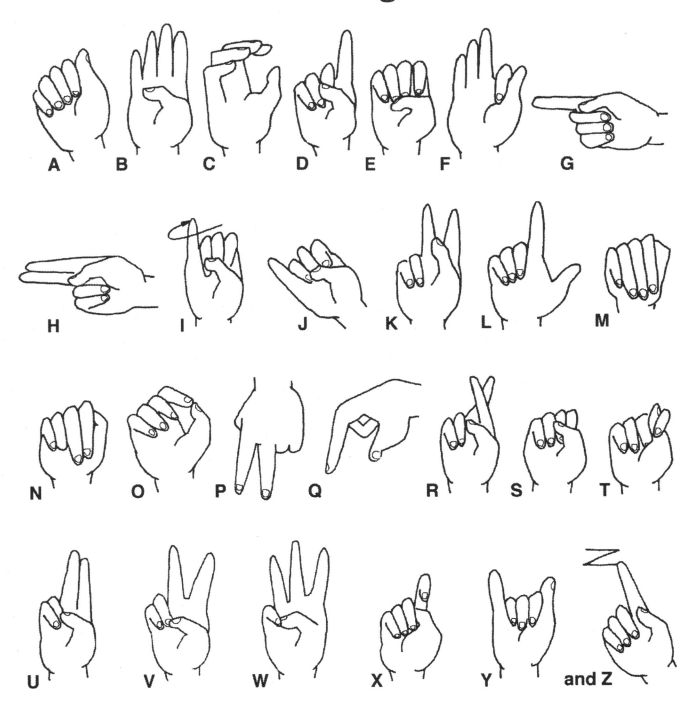

A   B   C   D   E   F   G

H   I   J   K   L   M

N   O   P   Q   R   S   T

U   V   W   X   Y   and Z

UNIT EIGHT: Hearing

One objective of this unit is to help a child to better understand and appreciate his or her sense of hearing. It will also help promote a better understanding of and respect for people who are deaf. As children learn more about their world and the people in it, there is much less of a chance for needless fear or debilitating prejudice to develop.

Sign Language will be used within this unit. However, it is very important to include Sign Language within every unit you do. It can be included in games, conversation, and music. Recent studies show that children who learn Sign (including non-deaf children) have better reading, observation, and fine-motor skills. In addition, learning Sign Language is fun, interesting, and can heighten self-esteem as the children develop their Sign Language skills.

Your sincere enthusiasm for learning new signs along with the children will show them that adults can also learn new things, and it is important enough to you that you are spending time learning it as well. Since hearing loss is a natural part of the human aging process, many elderly people are presently learning Sign Language as a better source of communication. Sign is also used by people who are not able to speak but have perfect hearing ability.

Once you begin doing Sign Language with your children regularly, be prepared for them to start asking you how to Sign many new words. A resource book to keep at your fingertips and keep up their enthusiasm would be *The Joy of Signing* by Lottie Riekehoff. Please see the Appendix for ordering information.

You may post pictures, either drawn or cut from old magazines, of many types of ears, both animal and human. Post a diagram of the inner ear, which you can obtain from antibiotic information flyers or posters. You can contact a pediatrician or ear, nose, and throat specialist to request these.

Obtain or borrow as many musical instruments as possible for this unit. Percussion and string instruments, such as drums, triangles, violins, and guitars, are great visual examples of vibration. This would be an ideal time to invite a guest musician to visit your class. Either an accomplished musician or another student musician would be fine.

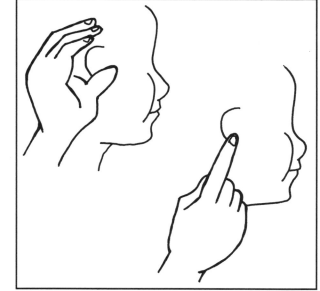

UNIT 8: HEARING

Date:

Dear Parents:

This week we will be discovering some fascinating facts about our "Sense of Hearing." We will find out how helpful it is to us and to animals. We will explore how our ears work and how sound travels through the air.

We will also be learning about deafness in order to help the children understand and respect people with sensory impairments. The more we know about things, the less frightening or "foreign" they become to us. Sign Language is a true language. It is not only a form of communication, but it is a fun learning experience. Learning to Sign strengthens memory, visual perception, and manual skills. Sign is fun to use in music, games, and conversation on a daily basis. Studies now show that children who learn Sign Language (including non-deaf children) have increased reading skills. They have also found that learning a second language, such as Sign, will make it easier to learn other languages.

At Home Ideas: Have a quiet time with your child in which you just sit and listen to sounds. Ask your child to show you some newly acquired Sign Language skills. Please use the attached sheet with a few signs on it to help your child remember some signs.

Learn more Sign Language yourself. Check out books on Sign Language at the library for yourself and your child, and make it a family project. A fun game to play with your child is to Sign something and have your child guess what you have Signed. There are many signs which are easy to guess, such as comb (run fingers through the hair) and baby (pretend to cradle a baby in your arms and sway them from side to side). Pantomime games which children love to play, such as charades, use body language - another form of Sign Language.

One great resource book filled with Sign Language used in everyday life is called *The Joy of Signing*, by Lottie L. Riekehoff. If you or someone you know would be interested in visiting our class to talk about a hearing impairment or ability with Sign Language, please let me know.

Sincerely,

ACTIVITY 73: Special Guest or Field Trip

Objectives: Respect for and understanding of deafness, and Sign Language skills.

Suggestions: Invite a deaf person or someone who speaks Sign Language to visit with your children. Contact a nearby Independent Living Center or a public school Special Education teacher. You should also be prepared to give the person a topic, or some ideas from your unit to discuss. For example, if you are teaching the children about animals, the person could come prepared to offer the children Sign Language skills on animals.

Tips: If you used the Sign Language in Activity 12 earlier in the unit on Africa, you might want to reintroduce this activity to refresh the children's memory. If the person needs for you to visit them, invite your children's parents along as chaperones it they are interested in learning more about Sign Language and hearing impairments.

bird

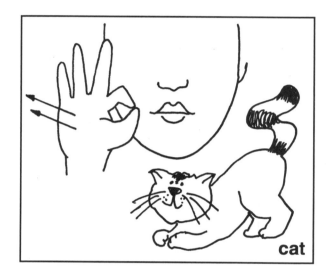

cat

duck

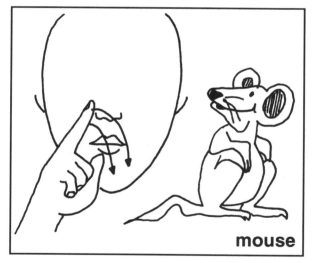

mouse

ACTIVITY 74: Teaching Sign Language

Objectives: Sign Language skills, memory skills, oral speech and language skills.

Preparation: The Sign Language in this publication may be photocopied for the children to take home and share with their families.

Please integrate Sign Language as well as many other languages within ALL weekly units on a daily basis. Sign can be used within storytelling and music, games, and conversation.

In the Appendix, there is an address and phone number provided for a company that makes a Sign Language alphabet poster, which would be an ideal learning tool for your classroom.

WITH RESPECT

ACTIVITY 75: Learning the Happy Birthday Song in Sign Language

Objectives: Music and rhythm skills, Sign Language skills, oral speech and language skills.

Tips: Please be respectful of other religions by not singing this song to children whose families do not celebrate birthdays. If the children cannot follow or do this activity, have them just repeat one sign throughout this entire song.

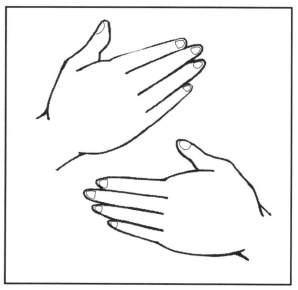

HAPPY

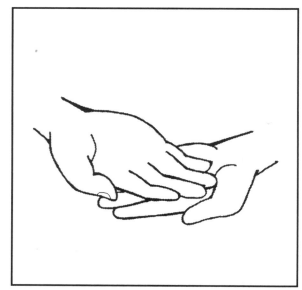

BIRTHDAY

TO

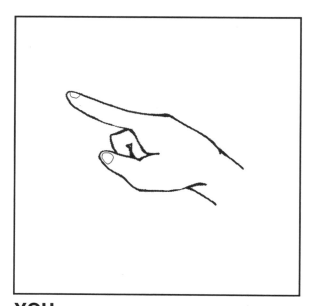

YOU

ACTIVITY 76: Read My Lips!

Objectives: Lip-reading and visual observation skills.

Materials:
- a television

Procedure: Many people with hearing impairments read lips to help them understand what other people are saying. Turn on the television to a program in which there is a close-up view of a person talking. Turn down the volume. Tell the children that this is what it would be like to watch t.v. if they were deaf. Ask the children to watch the mouth of the person talking to see if they can understand any of the words. Ask the children if this is easy to do. Tell them that it is a skill which takes much practice. Shut off the television and ask the children to look at your mouth and lip read while you speak. Mouth something such as, "I love you," very slowly and slightly exaggerating the movements of your mouth. Ask them what it is that you said to them.

Closed captioning is print at the bottom of the television which provides dialogue for hearing impaired persons. Tell the children about this and show them an example if possible.

Tips: If you have a videocassette player available, you might want to tape a talk show, or the news, and do this activity in slow motion. If you can tell what the person is saying, sound out each word slowly to help the children.

ACTIVITY 77: Hearing Aids

Objectives: Understanding deafness and the use of hearing aids.

Materials:
- a hearing aid or someone who wears one
- a radio, television, or cassette tape player

Procedure: If possible, borrow several types of hearing aids to show the children, or invite a person who wears a hearing aid to your class. Ask them to talk with the children about hearing aids. Ask your guest if they lip read. If so, ask how they acquired this skill. Your guest can share a song, story, or snack with your group. Tell the children that some people, but not all people, can be helped with hearing aids.

Using the radio, or a cassette player, allow the children to hear music at a low volume. Gradually turn up the volume to show how the hearing aid helps someone who can hear a slight bit. Then turn the sound all the way down, signifying total deafness. Allow the children to touch the hearing aid, and show them where and how it's worn.

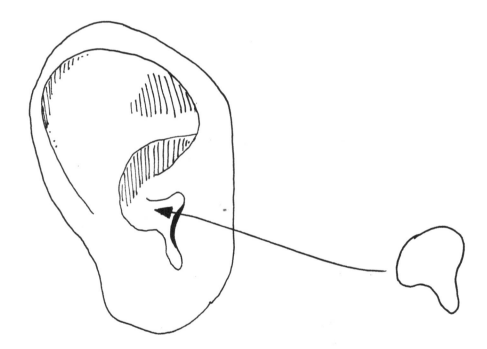

ACTIVITY 78: Drawing to Various Music and Sounds

Objectives: Artistic expression, emotional health, fine-motor and writing skills.

Materials:
- a blank cassette tape
- a tape recorder
- a wide variety of record albums or cassette tapes with different styles of music ranging from Classical to Rock
- several sheets of paper for each child
- crayons, pencils, pens, or markers

Procedure: Use the blank cassette to tape various pleasant and unpleasant noises and music. Play short segments of taped sounds and have the children draw to the sounds or music. They should use a new page of paper for each new sound. Be sure they use the backs of their paper in order to conserve.

Ask the Children: The sounds and noise levels that surround us can affect our moods and feelings. After finishing this activity, listen to the taped sounds again and ask each child to verbalize his or her feelings while listening. Is this a pleasant or unpleasant sound?

Tips: You could also conduct this activity using clay or Homemade Play Dough (see Activity 41). Also it is interesting to see how children interpret various ethnic musical selections. As this activity allows children free expression and a safe emotional outlet, you might want to try this activity throughout all your units, saving the artwork of each child to chart progress and skills.

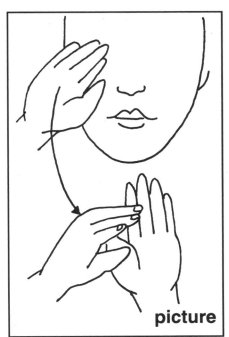

picture

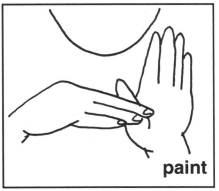

paint

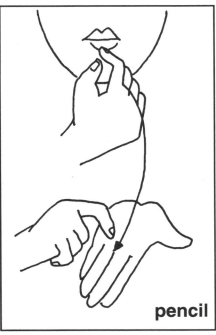

pencil

WITH RESPECT

ACTIVITY 79: What Changes Sound?

Objectives: Science and listening skills.

Materials:
- pots, plastic buckets, etc. (for drumming upon)
- wooden sticks and dowels
- a large metal spoon
- clothing to stuff into the buckets (for a muffling sound)
- a container of water to add to a metal pot

Procedure: Allow the children to tap on various containers to make sounds. Then have them fill their containers with an old shirt or other piece of heavy fabric. Have them drum on the containers again. Which was louder? Explain how the fabric absorbs and muffles the sound.

Fill a metal pot halfway with water. Have the children take turns tapping on the pot with a metal spoon while you move the pan from side to side. What does the moving water do to the sound waves traveling through it? Get ready for giggles!

Ask the Children: What would cars sound like without a noise muffler?

Tips: This activity shows how sound travels in waves and can be changed or distorted as it travels. You could also have the children cover their ears with their hands and strike the pot again. Explain how the waves didn't reach their ears, so they couldn't *hear* the noise.

ACTIVITY 80: Loud and Quiet

Objectives: Whole language and reading skills, sorting and observation skills.

Materials:
- two small pieces of posterboard
- a marker
- two tongue depressors
- masking tape

Preparation: Print the word, "Quiet" on one small piece of posterboard. Print the word, "Loud" on the other piece. Tape a tongue depressor onto each one, making signs with handles.

Procedure: Keep these words posted all week. Use them in many various ways such as:

- Play a game in which each time you make a noise, a child holds up either the "quiet" or the "loud" sign to identify the volume of the noise. This helps the children to recognize these printed words and connect them with meanings.

- If the children become excessively loud, hold up the sign which says, "Quiet." Don't say anything. See how long it takes them to notice the sign and become quiet.

- See the following activity in which you can hold up the signs corresponding with the volume/words.

ACTIVITY 81: A Chance to be Good and Loud! (A Chant)

Objectives: Group interaction skills, whole language and rhythm skills.

Materials:
• the "Loud" and "Quiet" signs from the preceding activity

Procedure: Hold up the "Loud" sign and as you clap on each word, yell in unison:
"Loud!—Loud!—
Loud, loud, loud!"
(repeat several times)

Next, when you hold up the "Loud" sign, have the children yell, "Loud, loud, loud!" very quickly in their own rhythm. Have them watch for you to hold up the "Quiet" sign to signal them to stop.

Hold up the "Quiet" sign and in unison whisper:
"Qui-et, qui-et, qui-et."

Then, when you hold up the "Quiet" sign, have them whisper the word, "Quiet" repeatedly at their own speed. Can you understand what is being said?

Tips: During your outdoor play, allow lots of noise. If excessive energy is not permitted indoors or outdoors, it can become bottled up within children. Many children have boisterous, loud personalities by nature. Enjoy allowing them to freely express who they are. Allow plenty of loud playtime for children each day. This activity and the signs can be used throughout the day to release energy, or to quiet the children down when they are too loud.

ACTIVITY 82: Animal Ears Hats

Objectives: Drawing, cutting, and dramatic play.

Materials:
- a half sheet of construction paper for each child
- construction paper cut into strips of one inch wide and long enough to fit around the children's heads
- markers
- scissors
- transparent tape

Procedure: Give each child a half sheet of construction paper. Have them draw the ears of their favorite animal onto their construction paper. (For younger children, assistance may be needed in drawing and/or cutting.) Next, the children can cut out their animal ears and tape them to a construction paper headband. Fasten the ends of the head bands with tape as you put them onto each child's head. Allow plenty of free playtime. If the hats can be used frequently for dramatic play, you may ask the children and parents to bring them back the following day to be used for more activities.

Ask the Children: What type of ears does a rabbit have – big or small? How about a bird? Can animals hear with their ears? How do they talk to each other? What do they do if they hear danger?

Tips: For ideas involving dramatic play, consult *Drama and Music: Creative Activities for Young Children.* See the Appendix for further information on this resource book.

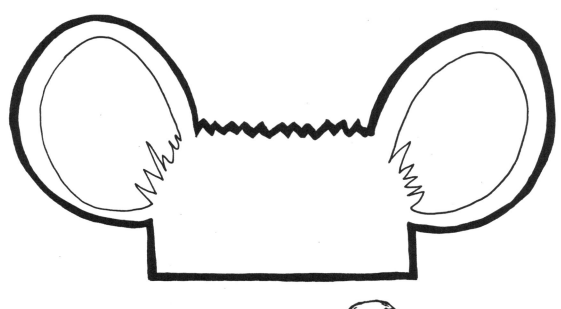

Animal Ear Patterns

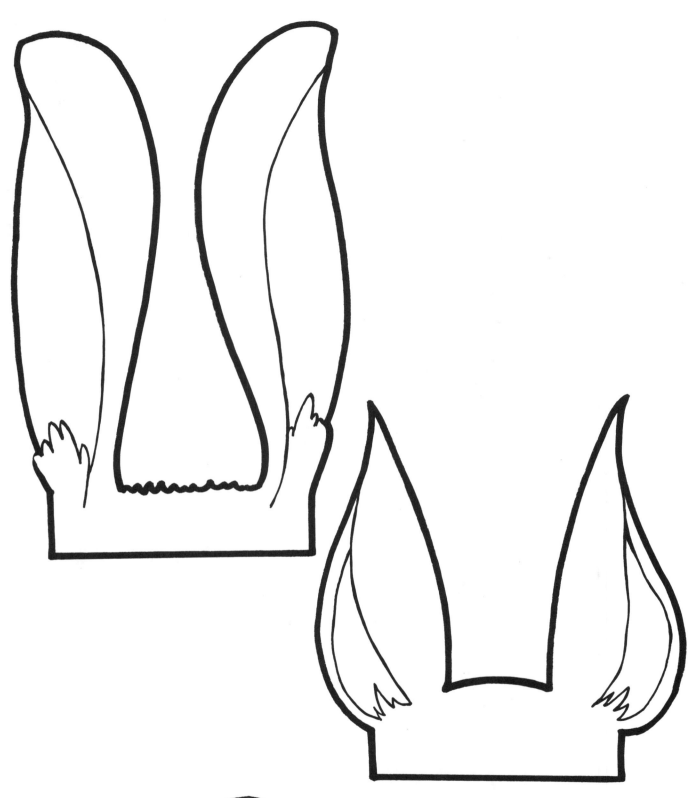

ACTIVITY 83: What Was That Sound?

Objectives: Auditory discrimination skills.

Materials:
- a tape recorder
- a blank cassette tape

Preparation: Tape record several different sounds, such as water running, a toilet flushing, a dog barking, someone biting into an apple, a musical instrument, a person whistling, a car horn, a car engine starting, and a vacuum cleaner.

Procedure: Play the tape for the children and have them identify the sounds. Have children make their own noises for the others to guess. Learning to distinguish sounds and copy sounds helps with listening skills and observational skills.

Ask the Children: What noises do you often hear in the classroom/kitchen/outside? What are some noises that animals make? What are some noises that people make? (Coughing, sneezing, footsteps, clapping, talking, snapping, etc.)

ACTIVITY 84: Sounds of Silence

Objectives: Sensory awareness, relaxation.

Procedure: Have the children lay on their backs on a soft location on the floor, or outdoors in the grass, and listen while they keep very quiet and still. It is helpful for the children to do this activity either immediately before nap time, since it will help relax them, or outdoors followed by outside play. This activity increases the children's awareness of the noises that surround them daily.

Ask the Children: To keep the children attentive and quiet, ask them to name at least three sounds that they can hear when you are finished being silent.

ACTIVITY 85: The Function of the Ear Drum (Tympanic Membrane)

Objectives: Scientific exploration.

Materials:
- a picture of an ear drum (Contact an ear, nose, and throat specialist to obtain this. They may have posters or diagrams and informational handouts.)
- a rubberband

Procedure: Show the children a picture of the ear drum. Next, attach the rubberband around two chair legs. Have the children take turns plucking the rubberband and watching it vibrate. Use the words "vibrate" and "vibration" often. Explain to the children that when a sound hits our ear drums it causes them to vibrate, enabling us to hear. Keep explanations minimal.

Tips: Plucking the rubberband at various lengths shows the children change in pitch. If your children are advanced enough to understand, explain how the tighter the rubberband is, the faster and higher pitch the vibration.

ACTIVITY 86: Sound Makers

Objectives: Listening skills, social and self-concept skills.

Procedure: Have each child take turns making a sound while the other children identify the sound. Make some sounds for the children to identify to start the game. Sounds could include motors, a jet plane engine, a siren, animal noises, a sneeze, a hiccup, a doorbell, etc. For social interaction, you could give one sound to two or three children and have them decide on how to make the noise. Also, you can divide children up into larger groups and try to come up with many noises for one item.

Ask the Children: How many different noises does a horse make? (Clop-clop-clop, Neigh, etc.) How many sounds can you make for a car? (Vrmmm, honk-honk, etc.)

Tips: Another way to play this activity is to tell a story to the children and have them all supply the noises as you read.

groarhh!   yodel la he hoo!   choo! choo!   mooooo!   neigh-he-he!   toot! toot!

Herman the dinosaur wanted to take a vacation. Herman

decided to go to the mountains by train.  On his way

to the mountains he saw a big field with cows  and

horses. The train let out a big whistle.

ACTIVITY 87: Sound Travels

Objectives: Science, auditory skills, and understanding sound waves.

Materials:
- two objects to hit together to make a loud noise
- a large space (this activity must be done in a large open outdoor area with at least 75-100 yards of space).

Procedure: Have an older child or another adult stand 75-100 yards away from you and the other children and hit two objects together loudly one time. Point out the time lapse between when you saw the objects being hit together and when you heard the noise. The children will be amazed at how long it takes for sound to travel.

ACTIVITY 88: Echoes

Objectives: Science, vocal exploration, understanding sound waves.

Materials: • a large space

Procedure: This activity also requires a large outdoor space and can be done in conjunction with the preceding activity. One location that works well for echoes is outside of a school building. The sound will bounce off the building and make an echo. The children will be fascinated - what a great opportunity to allow them to be loud!

Ask the Children: Where else have you heard on echo? (Cave, bathroom, hallway, auditorium, etc.)

UNIT NINE
Smell

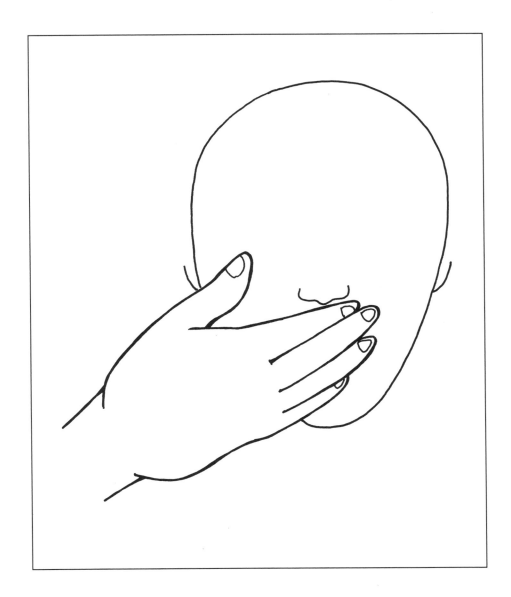

UNIT NINE: Smell

Children naturally investigate their world with their senses. We can further stimulate their interest by making their environment one in which sensory exploration is a daily occurrence.

During this unit, children will become more aware of their sense of smell. With awareness will come the appreciation of the important role our sense of smell has in our daily lives. From detecting dangerous smells, such as smoke or natural gas, to the sheer pleasure of fragrant flowers, our sense of smell is truly wondrous.

The fact that many people have a limited or nonexistent sense of smell should be shared with the children as information on other sensory impairments has been presented to them. Stress the ways people can use their many other abilities to lead normal, productive, meaningful lives despite impairments. It is important for children to become aware of and explore their own senses and the varying abilities of others in order to develop healthy, positive attitudes and relationships with people who are different from themselves.

A great number of people develop sensory and/or physical impairments later in life due to accidents, illnesses, or the natural aging process. Having your children interact regularly with the elderly (i.e. regular nursing home visits) will help build their awareness of this fact. This is only one of the MANY positive benefits to intergenerational activities.

For a free preschool smoking prevention package which includes activities, story booklets, stickers, and puppets, contact your state division of the American Cancer Society and request the preschool kit, "Starting Free, Good Air for Me."

UNIT NINE: Smell

Date:

Dear Parents:

This week our primary unit is the "Sense of Smell." We will be discovering how useful our sense of smell is, and how important it is to visually impaired people. We will also learn that not everyone has the sense of smell, and that it can temporarily disappear if we have a cold. We'll also find out which of our other senses could not exist without our sense of smell: our sense of taste.

In this unit the children will learn how different animals use their sense of smell, such as for locating food, finding lost people (bloodhounds), smelling and steering clear of danger, and finding a mate. We'll also learn about an animal which fends off its enemies with its ability to produce a strong-scented and irritating spray.

*Please send a small portion of one fragrant item with your child tomorrow in a tightly sealed container, such as an old margarine container. Some suggestions are: a cinnamon stick, scratch and sniff stickers or books, an orange peel, onion, peanut butter, coffee, garlic, juice, toothpaste, baking extract such as vanilla or mint, a flower, or surprise us with an idea of your own. These items will be used in several activities to build your child's awareness of different smells. Not only will the children try to guess, group, and match various smells, but they will also use these items in memory games, projects, and scientific explorations. I greatly appreciate your integral participation and help in collecting these materials.

At Home Ideas: Since we will be learning about smells that signal danger, it would be helpful to ask your child, "What types of smells are dangerous smells?"

Sincerely,

ACTIVITY 89: Who Knows – Whose Nose?

Objectives: Cognitive skills, introduction to sense of smell, and humor.

Materials:
- magazine pictures of people and animals (or draw your own)
- empty cereal boxes or posterboard
- glue or putty adhesive
- scissors

Preparation: Cut out just the noses, beaks, snouts, and trunks from pictures of animals and people. Glue all of the pictures onto cereal box pieces or posterboard. Trim off the cereal box or posterboard so that it is no longer visible around the photos. Place a small amount of adhesive to the back of each face and nose, and post them on the wall. Place the noses together in one group, and the faces in another.

Procedure: Have the children match each nose with the correct face. Allow them to have fun making silly combinations, such as a person with an elephant trunk.

Tips: Drawn or cartoon pictures work just as well, with less hassle than magazine pictures. A wide variety of noses also works the best.

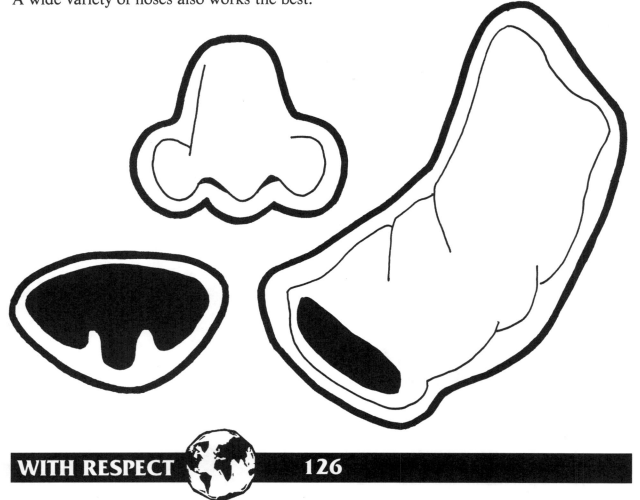

ACTIVITY 90: Bring a Favorite Scent

Objectives: Identification of scents, sensory discrimination.

Materials:
- the parent letter from this unit (photocopy one per child)
- masking tape
- a pen
- *optional:* eye covers

Procedure: Send home the parent letter with each child. The next day, have each child take turns carrying the scented item in his or her container to each of the other children. Allow the children to smell each item while closing their eyes, and then guess what it is. After guessing, they can open their eyes and see what is actually in the container.

Tips: You might want to have some scented items handy for children who do not bring one from home. For a more extended version of this exercise, please see the following activity.

ACTIVITY 91: Multi-Sensory Memory Game

Objectives: Nasal and visual skills, memory skills.

Materials:
- margarine containers, or any plastic opaque containers, with scented items from the previous activity
- masking tape
- markers

Preparation: Use masking tape and markers to write the children's names on the bottom of their containers.

Procedure: Pass out a container to each child (which is not their own) and have the children try to remember who brought it. Then they can look at the name on the bottom to see if they are correct. You can collect the containers, switch them around, and pass them out several different times repeating this activity. Allow the children to see and smell what is in the container to stimulate their memories sensorially.

Tips: If you have enough time, each time the children switch containers, have every child say whose container they received and what they brought. For example, "I have Daniel's container and he brought vanilla." This will reinforce the child's memory of each turn.

ACTIVITY 92: "Fragrant Field Trip" Suggestions

Objectives: Community awareness, sensory skills.

Suggestions: Phone a bakery and ask to arrange a tour for your children, allowing them to have a sample of freshly baked bread, a cookie, or other baked item. Ask what the cost per child will be. Stress that the tour be quite short, simple, and easy to understand. Ask to have the children visit when there is no danger of hot foods being removed from the oven.

Or, if you have botanical gardens located near you, phone the manager and make an appointment for a very simple tour for your children. Ask if the children will be permitted to smell different flowers as part of the tour. *A note on bees:* Most bees are attracted to people because of brightly-colored clothing, perfumes, or perfumed soaps. When a bee realizes that a person is not a flower, it will most often fly away. Inform the children of this and ask them to be still rather than swat at bees.

A restaurant tour is another option. Please consider any of the large selection of ethnic food restaurants. Again, remind the manager that if the children are allowed in the kitchen, you'd like it to be at a time when they aren't in any danger of sharp or hot objects.

ACTIVITY 93: Six Senses Song

My "Six" Senses

Teacher: I can smell, smell a rose.
Tell me, tell me, what do I smell with?
I can smell, smell a rose.
What do I use to smell?

Children: Your nose.

Teacher: I can hear, hear a bird.
Tell me, tell me, what do I hear with?
I can hear, hear a bird.
What do I use to hear?

Children: Your ears.

Teacher: I can taste, taste an orange.
Tell me, tell me, what do I taste with?
I can taste, taste an orange.
What do I use to taste?

Children: Your mouth.

Teacher: I can touch, touch my dog.
Tell me, tell me, what do I touch with?
I can touch, touch my dog.
What do I use to touch?

Children: Your hands.

Teacher: I can see, see my friends.
Tell me, tell me, what do I see with?
I can see, see my friends.
What do I use to see?

Children: Your eyes.

Teacher: I can dream, I can dream.
Tell me, tell me, what do I dream with?
I can dream, I can dream.
What do I use to dream?

Children: Your imagination.

Tips: Music for this song can be found on the audio cassette, *Music With Respect, Volume 1-2P*. See Appendix for ordering information.

ACTIVITY 94: Smell Book

Objectives: Sensory and memory skills, and fostering a love of books.

Materials for each child:
- four fragrant items in powder form(such as ground cinnamon, oregano, garlic or onion powder, talcum powder, toothpaste, or baking extracts)
- five small plastic lids
- four milk lids
- glue
- paint brushes or cotton swabs
- a 10" piece of yarn
- a zip seal bag

Materials for the teacher:
- a hole punch
- a permanent marker
- sharp scissors

Preparation: Cut off the outer ridge from each plastic lid. Place a little of each fragrant item in a milk lid for each child.

Procedure: Give each child five plastic lids, their four milk lids, glue, and a brush or cotton swab. Have the children place a small amount of glue on each margarine lid, and sprinkle a small amount of each fragrant item onto the glue. Combining the scents should be allowed. Allow them to select the scents that they would like to use.

After the glue is dry, punch two holes in each margarine lid and bind each child's set of lids with yarn to make a book. A title such as "Smell Book" or "Smells" can be printed with permanent marker. Allow the marker to dry before the children use their books.

Tips: If the children wish to take their "Smell Books" home, seal them in ziplock bags first. If you do not have access to many plastic lids, cardboard squares, circles, or triangles work just as well. You may wish to incorporate shape identification in this activity, as well, cutting all different shapes for each child.

Tell the children that there are many people whose noses cannot smell things even though they may be very capable of hearing, seeing, and feeling things.

ACTIVITY 95: I Smell Danger (Puppet Show)

Objectives: Safety, dramatic play.

Materials:
- two puppets - a parent and a child (paper bags or sock puppets are fine)
- a scratch and sniff card with natural gas odor on it. These are easily obtained from most gas companies. Call and request that some be sent to your school, preferably one per child.

Puppet Show: The child puppet's parent rests on the couch. The child puppet walks into the kitchen and smells a very bad and unusual odor. The child puppet tells her parent about the smell. The parent hurries to the kitchen to see that one of the burners on the stove was left slightly turned on to allow gas to escape. The parent puppet shuts off the stove and takes the child puppet outside, leaving the door open to ventilate the house.

The parent puppet gives the child much praise for reporting the strange smell. The puppets can then tell the audience, "If you ever smell a bad odor such as smoke (like something is burning) or gas, tell a grownup right away."

Then give each child a natural gas scented card to take home and share with their parents.

Tips: This activity provides an excellent opportunity for you to reinforce fire safety lessons with the children.

Finger Puppet Patterns

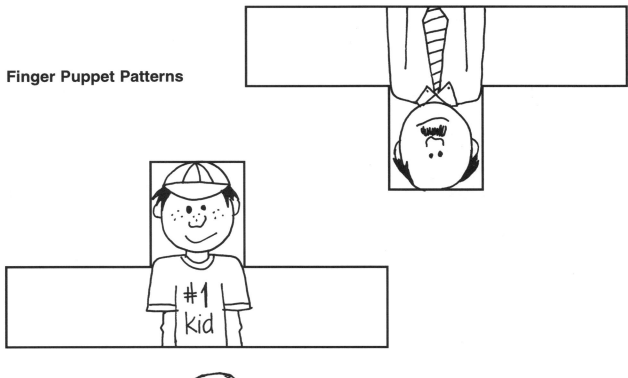

ACTIVITY 96: Can Taste Exist Without Smell?

Objectives: Scientific observation, learning about the sense of smell.

Procedure: At a snack or meal time, have the children pinch their noses closed and take a bite of food.

Ask the Children: Can you taste the food? Have them unplug their noses. Ask, "Now can you taste your food? What if you had a cold in your nose and couldn't smell anything - could you taste food then? When you smell your favorite food, can you almost taste it?

Tips: You might want to prepare for some questions on this activity, the children will be amazed that it actually works.

ACTIVITY 97: Bloodhound Game

Objectives: Differentiating and matching scents, memory skills.

Materials:
- two empty opaque plastic containers for each scent
- small paper napkins to cover each container
- transparent tape
- one strongly scented item for each child, such as vegetable peels, cucumber, onion, garlic, flowers, a small pine branch, baking extracts, perfume, or toothpaste.

Preparation: Divide each scent into halved amounts. Place each of the halves into a separate container. Keep one of each of the scented items on a table, and place the other containers on the floor in a large circle. Cover each scented item with a small piece of paper napkin taped over the container.

Procedure: Give each child at the table a scented item to smell. Have the children pretend to be bloodhounds and hunt for the matching scent container on the floor by crawling on hands and knees, sniffing each item in the circle. When a child thinks he or she has found the matching item, have them bring it back to the table to make sure. At this time they can peek inside the containers.

Tell the children that groups of bloodhounds can often smell an item which has a person's scent on it. They can also find people or things which are lost in a forest.

Ask the Children: If you couldn't smell, how else could you find the matching scent? (Sight, touch, asking an adult, etc.)

ACTIVITY 98: What's Cooking?

Objectives: Sensory identification skills

Preparation: Before the children arrive, bake bread or muffins. Frozen loaves of dough are a quick, inexpensive method.

Procedure: As the children arrive, ask them to guess what they smell. Write down their guesses, and tell the children that they will all find out what the smell is together. After all of the children have arrived and guessed what the smell is, read all of the guesses without revealing who guessed what. Then show the children what food was making the scent.

Allow the children to enjoy eating this special treat together.

Tips: Explain to the children that smells travel through the air, just like sounds.

ACTIVITY 99: Dog Scents (Puppet Show)

Objectives: Science, safety, dramatic play, and humor.

Materials:
- a dog puppet or stuffed toy
- a skunk puppet or stuffed toy
- a person puppet or doll

Puppet Show Suggestions: The dog puppet, says, "Ruff! I smell my dinner coming." A person puppet brings in a pretend bowl of dog food. The person puppet can wait until the dog is finished eating to pet it saying, "I'd better wait till my dog Fido is finished eating before I pet him. Otherwise, he might get upset or angry and think I'm trying to take away his food."

Then the person can pet the dog. The dog puppet can say, "Ruff! I love to smell my person - but wait! I smell another dog on my person! My person must have been petting another dog today!"

The person goes away from the dog, and the dog sneaks out the door of the house which was left open. The dog smells its way through the neighborhood. Its nose leads it to some food on the ground which he eats. *Remind the children never to eat food they find on the ground.* Then it smells a rabbit and chases it, but doesn't catch it. Then the dog sees a skunk and starts to chase it. Instead of running away, the skunk senses danger, lifts its tail and sprays the dog. The dog runs home to its person, smelling like skunk. The person smells the dog and says, "Uh-oh Fido! You smell like a skunk!! Time for a bath!"

Ask the Children: Have you ever smelled a skunk? Do they smell good or bad? If you see or smell a skunk, what should you do? (Go find an adult right away.)

ACTIVITY 100: Elephant Noses

Objectives: Scientific discovery.

Materials:
- a picture or drawing of an elephant
- several fragrant items
- a large space, inside

Preparation: Explain to the children that elephants can smell things up to several hundred yards away. Elephants have very poor vision, so their sense of smell is very important to them.

Procedure: Show the children approximately how far away an elephant can detect smells. Experiment with the distance within which the children can detect smells.

Ask the Children: Why is the sense of smell important? (Sensing danger.) Would the wind change our ability to smell things outdoors? Do you think elephants can smell very well? What makes you think so?

ACTIVITY 101: Slither, Slither Snake (Poem/Song)

Objectives: Science exploration, speech, and language skills.

Here's a tongue twister song about an animal that smells with its tongue. If you've ever held a non-poisonous pet snake and saw its tongue darting out of its mouth over your skin, you were being "smelled" by the snake.

Slither, Slither Snake

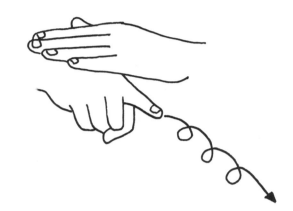

Slither, slither snake.
Slither, slither snake.

You smell the air with your long tongue.
Watching you is so much fun.

Slither, slither snake.
Slither, slither snake.

Tips: Explain again how closely taste and smell are linked by referring to Activity 96. During the lines which say "slither, slither," have the children squirm and wriggle like little squirming snakes.

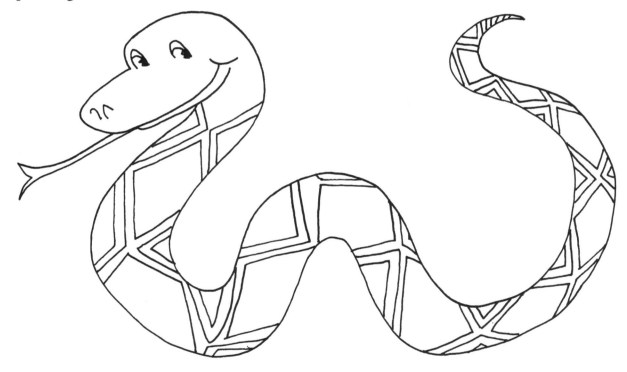

UNIT TEN
Sight

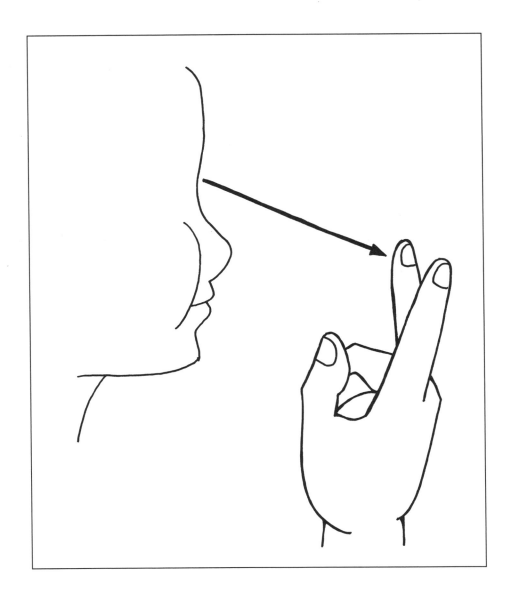

WITH RESPECT

UNIT TEN: Sight

A young child's observation and visual skills are often very sharp. An adult can bring a child to a store for the first time and he or she may point out things which were never noticed by the adult before. Children have such a zest for discovering new things and places that they naturally are very skilled observers. This doesn't mean that they have the attention skills to match, nor would we expect them to.

A child's visual memory can be challenged and improved upon. Activities which do this are appropriate not only during this week, but regularly. Memory games may be involved, such as using a few pairs from a deck of cards and having the children attempt to select matched pairs when the cards are facing down. Memory games could also be as simple as making a change on yourself, such as wearing your shirt backwards, your hair in a different way, or wearing your shoes on the wrong feet. (You'd better hope they figure that one out right away!) Or, you can change or rearrange some of the toys or furniture in the room. Tell the children to be alert, and be detectives throughout this unit to watch for things that have been changed.

Sign Language is also an excellent way to improve one's visual observation skills. Children are naturally talented at deciphering body language. Many times if we need their attention, we don't need to say a word to relay a message. Try to incorporate Sign Language regularly, along with using facial expressions and body language. Most children cannot imagine not being able to see. The best way to promote acceptance and understanding of visual impairment is to have a blind visitor interact with your children. Since sight loss is common with age, it is important for children not to fear or avoid those with visual impairments, but to appreciate their perseverance and ingenuity in a visually-oriented world.

If you do not have any Braille storybooks for your children to use on a regular basis, please invest in one. Every preschool should have at least one! See the resources in the appendix for more information, or see Activity 106: Touching Braille, for instructions on how to simulate Braille for the children.

UNIT TEN: Sight

Date:

Dear Parents:

This week our primary topic will be the "Sense of Sight." We will find out about people who can't see as we do, and how these people function with great capability and independence, and develop their many abilities. In one of our activities, we'll pretend we cannot see. We'll also be touching Braille, discovering the job of seeing-eye dogs, and find out about and try White Canes. We will see what it would be like to be a blind artist and will learn that there are many outstanding blind artists in the world.

Some activities in this unit will teach the children about sight and the eye with tools such as magnifying glasses, prisms, and binoculars. The children will be involved in many activities which will improve visual memory and visual observation skills, as well.

At Home Ideas: You can help your children to better comprehend the concepts of sight and blindness by having them try to find his or her way through your home with their eyes covered. Have them avoid stairs and be sure to remove all potential hazards and obstacles before starting. Make sure your child only tries this under your supervision.

If anyone in your family wears glasses or contact lenses, show the child how they're used, why they're used, and how to clean and care for them.

Sincerely,

ACTIVITY 102: Let's See What You See

Objectives: Observation skills, sensory identification, and appreciation of different visual abilities and perspectives.

Materials:
- A chair

Procedure: Have each child sit in the chair looking straight ahead. Ask them to call out everything they can see without turning their head. Next, have the child stand on the chair and repeat the activity. Can the child see more things, different things, less things? Children learn how to look for details in this activity, becoming more aware of their environment. Explain to the children that everyone sees things differently, even if they're the same height. Help them to understand that each and every person on earth has his or her own unique perspective.

Ask the Children: What could you do differently if you were this tall? What could you no longer do?

Tips: Place favorite toys, pictures, or objects on shelves, or up high for better results. If a child does not see anything new, you can have them turn around and name things or move the chair to a different location.

ACTIVITY 103: No Peek Pictures

Objectives: Introduction to blind artists, fine-motor and tactile skills.

Materials:
- a large sheet of paper for each child
- a choice of washable non-toxic markers, crayons, or paints
- eye covers

Procedure: Have children wear their eye covers. Please see Activity 57: Touching with Covered Hands, for instructions on how to make these. Allow children to color with markers or crayons, or paint on their sheets of paper pretending to be blind artists. You may wish to play music or read a story out loud as the children do this activity.

Tips: To save tying time before each use of the eye covers, have the children remove them while keeping them tied. If a child does not feel comfortable wearing the eye covers, they may participate with their eyes closed.

ACTIVITY 104: Pretending to Be Blind

Objectives: Sensory skills and understanding blindness.

Materials:
- eye covers

Preparation: Remove obstacles and block all stairways. Make sure there are no sharp or protruding objects for children to run into or knock over.

Procedure: Have the children wear eye covers for a short time in order to achieve a better appreciation and understanding of what blindness is. Please see Activity 57 for instructions on how to make these. Explain to them that people who are blind see only darkness when their eyes are open and not covered. Many children think that blindness can be cured by opening one's eyes. Tell the children that people who are blind almost always stay blind, but that they can be active, productive, independent people!

Tips: Music by Ray Charles, Stevie Wonder, or any of the very accomplished blind musicians would be an excellent choice this week. Check at your public library. Also, allow the children to play various instruments wearing eye covers.

ACTIVITY 105: Invite a Blind Person to Visit

Objectives: Understanding blindness, and respect for the capabilities and independence of blind people.

Suggestions: You may wish to have your guest read a story in Braille, tell a story, have a snack, sing a song, or play a musical instrument. Ask them to share one of their talents or interests, or just come to talk and play with the children.

Before your guest arrives, ask the children to name some games or activities they enjoy that do not rely upon vision, i.e.: singing songs, fingerpainting, listening to stories, guessing games, playing with clay or play dough, etc.

Tips: Consider inviting a visitor who is of the children's age level, as well. Interacting with peers of differing abilities builds respect and understanding. Contact a nearby School for the Blind, Special Education teacher, Independent Living Center, or Council of the Blind for more information.

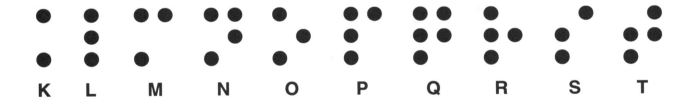

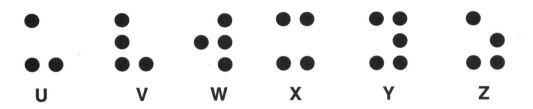

WITH RESPECT

ACTIVITY 106: Watching Pupils Change Size

Objectives: Scientific observation, understanding the eye.

Materials:
- eye covers
- small hand mirrors (one per child or small group of children)

Procedure: Have children wear eye covers and remove them quickly in front of hand mirrors to watch their pupils contract and dilate. Explain how the pupil changes size in order to allow the proper amount of light into the eye. In this activity, children learn how complex and fragile eyesight is.

Tips: If this method does not produce results, have one child observe as another child looks straight ahead. Making sure not to shine directly into the eye, take a flashlight and turn it on and off quickly in front of the second child. Be prepared to answer questions with this activity, children are fascinated with this "trick of the eye."

ACTIVITY 107: Touching Braille

Objectives: Tactile skills, and appreciation for Braille print.

Materials:
- books or periodicals printed in Braille which may be found at your public library. Please make the investment of purchasing Braille storybooks for your children to use regularly! Or, you could simulate your own Braille.

To simulate Braille you need:
- paper
- a ball point pen
- a magazine or other soft cover book

Procedure: Place a sheet of paper on a soft cover magazine or book. The children can press the ball point pen onto the paper firmly several times in order to make Braille-like patterns. When you turn the paper over, the indentations made by the pen will feel like Braille. Then they can turn over their papers, close their eyes, and let their fingertips glide across the page to feel genuine Braille or simulated Braille. This will help them understand how people without sight can read.

Tips: Braille can be found in public places also such as in elevators, on soft drink lids from fast food restaurants, and on the outside of motel room doors. The children can spell their names in simulated Braille by looking for the letters on Braille alphabet cards and copying the letter patterns, as described previously. To purchase Braille alphabet cards, contact the National Federation of the Blind, listed in the Appendix.

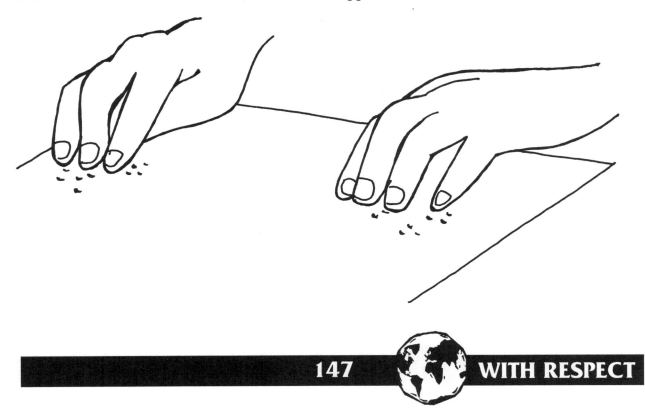

WITH RESPECT

ACTIVITY 108: Seeing-Eye Dogs

Objectives: Social skills, understanding and appreciation of seeing-eye dogs.

Materials:
- eye covers

Preparation: Remove all obstacles and dangerous items from the room and block all stairways.

Procedure: To show the children how blind people can live independent lives with the help of seeing-eye dogs, have the children get into groups of two. One child can pretend to be the dog (but must remain standing upright), and the other child can wear the eye covers, pretending to be blind. See Activity 57 for how to make these. The child who is pretending to be the dog can lead the other child around the room.

Ask the Children: Did you feel safer with the help of a pretend dog, or when you were on your own as in previous activities?

Tips: You may wish to contact your local Council of the Blind for some information on seeing-eye dogs and how they are trained.

ACTIVITY 109: What Color Are Our Eyes?

Objectives: Visual observation skills, memory skills, and artistic expression.

Materials:
- mirrors (one for each child or group of children)
- paper
- markers, crayons, and colored pencils

Procedure: Have each child look in a mirror to see what color his or her eyes are. The children may say, "Black," even if they have blue eyes, since they may only notice the pupil. If so, help them to determine their eye color. Then ask them to look at their friends' eyes and see how their eyes look, and what colors they are.

Now ask the children to draw a picture of a friend remembering what their eyes looked like. Some children may just choose a color (such as brown) and color the whole sheet of paper that color because it reminds them of the eyes they just saw. That's fine! Each drawing can be as unique as each child.

Ask the Children: What things are the same about all of our eyes? What things are different about our eyes? Everyone's eyes are very special, unique, and different. Even if there are many people with brown eyes, those people will not have exactly the same eyes.

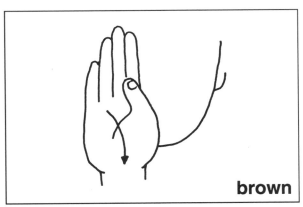
brown

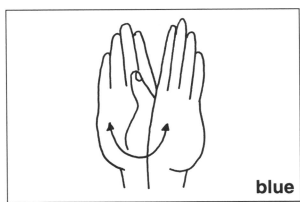
blue

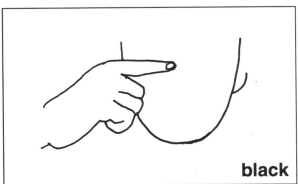
black

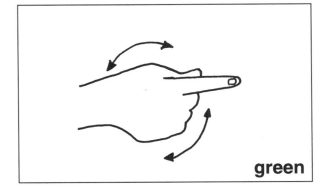
green

WITH RESPECT

ACTIVITY 110: Whose Eyes?

Objectives: Visual identification skills, memory skills.

Materials for the teacher:
- a large, flat piece of cardboard (about 3'x5')
- a sharp instrument such as an Exacto knife

Preparation: Cut a rectangular hole in the cardboard which will be the right size for only a child's eyes to show through.

Procedure: Allow half of the children to hide behind the piece of cardboard. Have one of those children peek through the hole in the cardboard. The children on the other side then try to identify whose eyes they see. Take turns allowing each child a turn to look through the hole while the others guess who it is.

Tips: This activity is most successful when it is done directly after the previous activity, where the children were asked to observe their friends' eye colors. Another way to play a guessing game involving memory skills would be the following: have the children take turns trying to guess who is in front of them by just touching their face and hair. Or, have one child close his or her eyes while the other children take turns speaking to them. These further activities involve both the sense of touch and hearing, and help the children to rely less on their sense of sight.

ACTIVITY 111: A White Cane

Objectives: Understanding of White Canes and sensory exploration.

Materials:
- eye covers
- a White Cane (borrowed from a local division of a Council of the Blind)
- OR you can make your own: the cane, or walking stick, should be solid white or white trimmed with red

This activity must be done in a large open space on level ground, such as an outdoor location. If you don't have this kind of space, it's best to demonstrate this activity yourself while the children watch.

Procedure: Allow each child to feel and hold the stick and then pass it to another child. Then, one at a time, cover the children's eyes and have them walk a short distance both without the stick and then with the stick to conclude which way was the best.

Ask the Children: How could a White Cane help a person who cannot see?

Tips: Many states have laws for people who are carrying a White Cane. One of these laws prohibits a vehicle from getting closer than ten feet to a person carrying a White Cane while it is in an extended position. Explain the difference between White Canes and walking canes to the children.

ACTIVITY 112: Stimulating the Sense of Sight

Objectives: Visual identification skills, observation skills.

Materials:
  • hidden picture books or picture search books.
  (An example would be *I Spy* by Jean Marzollo)

Procedure: Allow the children to look at the books to find the hidden pictures on their own. They love to help each other with this activity.

Tips: Other ways to make great use of a child's sense of sight include search games such as Hide and Seek and Hide the Penny. Depending on the children's ages, you might want to hide many objects, larger and easier to locate than a penny.

ACTIVITY 113: Binoculars

Objectives: Scientific exploration, visual identification skills.

Materials:
- two empty cardboard bathroom tissue tubes per child
- yarn
- a hole punch

Procedure: You can make a pair of binoculars for each child. Allow them to decorate them with paint or markers however they wish. Go on a nature walk and each time you stop, allow the children to look through the binoculars. For safety purposes, insist that they stop walking before looking through the binoculars.

Tips: You could also borrow or purchase a pair of real or plastic binoculars for the children to look through as well.

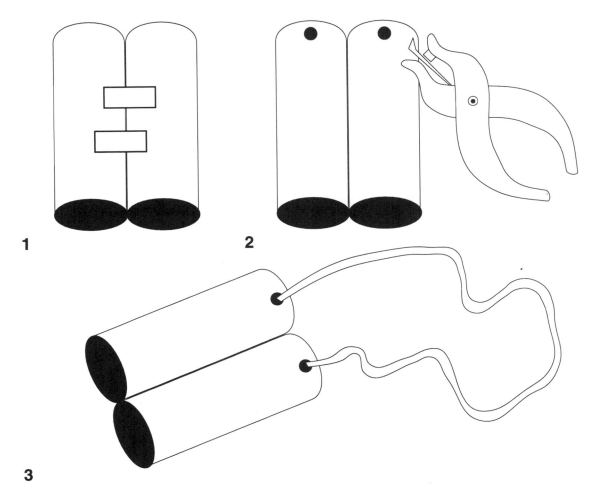

1

2

3

ACTIVITY 114: Visual Memory

Objectives: Memory skills, visual identification skills.

Materials:
- a tray
- ten different objects
- a piece of fabric to cover objects on the tray

Procedure: Place three objects on the tray. Cover the objects. Ask a child to tell you what was on the tray. Add more objects each time the child remembers them all.

Alternate Suggestion: Place several objects the tray. Secretly remove one. Ask the child, "What is missing?"

Tips: If the child cannot remember the object(s), give them clues to stimulate their visual memory. If this does not work, allow them to feel the object under the fabric and guess again.

ACTIVITY 115: Colors

Objectives: Visual stimulation, scientific exploration, understanding of colors.

Materials:
- a piece of heavy white paper, or white cardboard cut into a circle
- a marker
- tempera paints

Procedure: Show the class a color wheel with the three primary colors painted in: yellow, red, and blue. Then, as the children observe, mix orange, purple, and green paint (using the primary colors) and paint in the orange, purple, and green sections of the color wheel. Tack the finished color wheel on the bulletin board. Give the children small color wheels to paint and take home.

Ask the Children: Can you point out things around the classroom that are green? Blue?

Tips: On an observation walk, have the children collect things which are green, brown, red, yellow, round, or pointed.

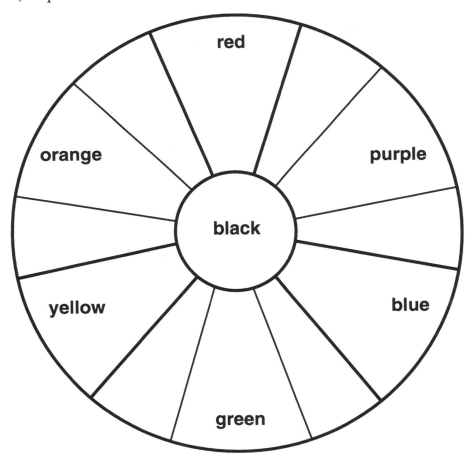

WITH RESPECT

ACTIVITY 116: Imagination T.V.

Objectives: Stimulation of sense of hearing, appreciation for blindness, listening and imaginative skills.

Materials:
- a television
- eye covers

Procedure: After picking out a suitable program for the children to watch, have them try to figure out what's going on by just listening. To achieve this, either dim the image on the T.V. or have the children wear their eye covers. Please see Activity 57 for how to make these.

Ask the Children: What are the people/animals doing? What do you think this character looks like? Is that person happy or sad? How can you tell?

Tips: If you do not have access to a television, a story on record or tape will work also. With a videotape or cassette tape it is easier to stop and ask the children questions frequently.

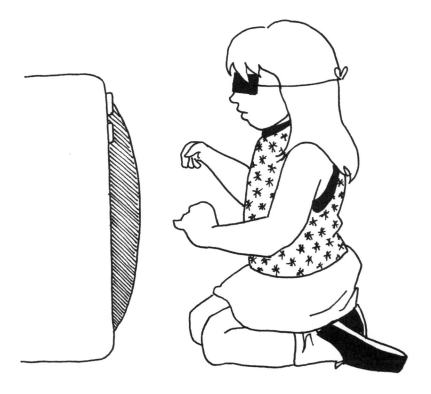

ACTIVITY 117: Acting in the Dark

Objectives: Listening and imaginative skills, appreciation for blindness, gross-motor skills, and dramatic play.

Materials:
- a storybook, preferably one with lots of action
- eye covers
- a large, open space

Preparation: Clear an open space of obstacles and potential hazards.

Procedure: Depending upon the size of the class and skills of the children, you may not want them to wear eye covers during this activity. As the children listen to a story, have them imagine in their minds what the characters are doing. When the story is over, have the children act out small parts of the action.

Ask the Children: Show me how this character walks. How did you know that?

Tips: Instead of a storybook read aloud, you could do this activity by playing Simon Says with words only. If done with the eye covers on, this activity builds body awareness, muscle coordination, memory skills, and an appreciation for both the limitations and the unique capabilities of those without sight.

APPENDIX

General Multicultural Resources

Acazar Records. P.O. Box 429, Waterbury, VT 05676. (800)541-9904. Call to place credit card orders or to receive a catalog. A sturdy, hardboard big-book children's atlas entitled *It's a Big, Big World* which includes a cassette is available.

Creative Thoughts & Surplus Stuff. (800)886-6428. Call to place credit card orders or to receive a catalog. Multicultural modeling clay is available in four skin-tones, ask for item #632.

Hodges-Caballero, Jane, Ph.D. *Children Around the World: A Multicultural Journey.* Atlanta, GA: Humanics Learning, 1994.

MCC Selfhelp Crafts. 500 Main Street, Akron, PA 17501. (717)859-4971. Contact to receive a retail catalog of handmade crafts and musical instruments from people in developing countries, including Mexico and some countries in Africa.

Music With Respect, Volumes 1 and 2. Wisconsin: Quality Instructional Publications, 1992. Call (800)841-4294 to place your order.

Multicultural Publishers' Exchange. (800)558-2110. Call to receive a free catalog of publications written by and about people of various races and cultures.

SERRV Selfhelp Handcrafts. 21 South 12th Street, P.O. Box 365, New Windsor, MD 21776. (301)635-2255. Contact to receive a retail catalog of handmade crafts and musical instruments from people in developing countries, including Mexico and some countries in Africa.

UNIT ONE: Self-Empowerment & Self-Esteem

Magellan, Mauro. *Cambio Chameleon.* Atlanta, GA: Humanics Children's House, 1990.

Magellan, Mauro. *Home at Last.* Atlanta, GA: Humanics Children's House, 1990.

Neuman, Susan, Ph.D and Renee Panoff, Ph.D. *Exploring Feelings.* Atlanta, GA: Humanics Learning, 1983.

Rose, Angie, Ph.D and Lynn Weiss, Ph.D. *Self-Esteem Activities: Giving Children From Birth to Six Freedom to Grow.* Atlanta, GA: Humanics Learning, 1994.

UNIT TWO: African Cultural Aspects

The African News Cookbook - African Cooking for Western Kitchens. Penguin Books, Copyright Africa News Service, 1985.

American Gourd Society. Box 274, Mt. Gilead, OH 43338-0274. Write for information on obtaining gourd seeds.

Braswell, Lena. Rt. 1, Box 73, Wrens, GA 30833. (404)547-6784. Contact to purchase dried gourds.

Feelings, Muriel and Tom. *Jambo Means Hello.* Dial Press, 1974.

Fisher, Linda. Rt. 1, Box 282, Nashville, NC 27856. (919)443-0715. Contact to purchase dried gourds.

Learning Through Movement. 570 N. Arden Blvd., Los Angeles, CA 90004. (212)460-4387. Dance-a-Story, Sing-A-Song - Early Childhood Multicultural Cassette. A multicultural children's music cassette which contains an African game/song from Ghana, an African American call and response song, and music and stories from other countries. Includes lyrics and movement instructions.

McCubbin, Boris. 508 Cappy Dr., Knoxville, TN 37920. Call to order gourd seeds, literature sheets sent free upon request with each order. Includes information on shapes and sizes of 50 gourds. Also available is information on growing and/or how to cure gourds.

Oriental Trading Co. (800)228-2269. Call to place credit card order for rolls of 100 African Stickers, ask for item #12-713.

UNIT THREE: Mexican Cultural Aspects

Manana Para Los Ninos. P 1985 Machete Records, C 1989 EarthBeat! (A Division of Music for Little People), P.O. Box 1460, Redway, CA 95560. Contact for a cassette of Mexican songs for children.

Ronstadt, Linda. "Canciones de mi Padre." Elektra/Asylum Records: 1987. This cassette can be found in (or ordered by) the following record stores: Musicland, SamGoody, and Discount Records.

UNIT FOUR: French Cultural Aspects

Blackwood, Alan and Brigitte Chosson. *France.* New York: The Bookwright Press, 1988.

Norbrook, Dominique. *Passport to France.* New York: Franklin Watts Ltd., 1994.

UNIT FIVE: Amish Cultural Aspects

Adams, Marcia. *Cooking from Quilt Country.* Clarkson N. Potter, Inc., 1989. Recipe for Amish Brown Sugar Pie reprinted with permission.

Coleman, Bill. *Amish Odyssey: Book of Photography.* St. James Press, 1988.

UNIT SIX: Touch

Brandenberg, Aliki. *My Five Senses.* New York: Thomas Y. Crowell Junior Books, 1989.

Ward, Brian R. *Touch, Taste and Smell.* New York: Franklin Watts Ltd., 1982.

UNIT SEVEN: Taste

Pluckrose, Henry. *Think About Tasting, Think About Touching, Think About Smelling.* (A Series) New York: Franklin Watts Ltd., 1986.

UNIT EIGHT: Hearing

Riekehoff, Lottie. *The Joy of Signing.* Missouri: Gospel Publishing House, 1987. (800)641-4310. Call to place credit card orders, order #020520. Hardcover, 352 pages.

Judy Instructo/American Teaching Aids. 4424 W. 78th St., Bloomington, MN 55435. (800)423-6537. Call to place a credit card order for a Sign Language alphabet poster, ask for item #ATA-1711. Or, to save on shipping costs, contact your local school supply store and ask them to order it for you.

UNIT NINE: Smell

American Cancer Society. Contact your state division for a free preschool smoking prevention package which includes activities, story booklets, stickers, and puppets. Request the preschool kit, "Starting Free, Good Air for Me."

UNIT TEN: Sight

National Federation of the Blind. 1800 Johnson St., Baltimore, MD 21230. (410)659-9314. Braille alphabet cards are available at a low cost with free shipping. Call to place credit card orders or send check. The items listed below are also available at this address at no cost, provided by the National Organization of Parents of Blind Children. When you call, also request these free items:
- Braille Storybook Resource List
- A Flier, The Blind Child in a Regular Preschool
- Booklets of personal stories of blind individuals. These can be adapted for preschool level.

Related Resource Books

Commins, Elaine, M.Ed. *Early Childhood Activities: A Treasury of Ideas from Worldwide Sources.* Atlanta, GA: Humanics Learning, 1982.

Knight, Michael, Ph.D and Terry Graham, M.A. *Science Activities Pre-K Through 3: Leaves Are Falling in Rainbows.* Atlanta, GA: Humanics Learning, 1995.

Manthey, Cynthia. *Pre-K Math: Concepts from Global Sources.* Atlanta, GA: Humanics Learning, 1995.

Rubin, Janet and Margaret Merrion. *Drama and Music: Creative Activities for Young Children.* Atlanta, GA: Humanics Learning, 1995.

Trencher, Barbara R., M.S. *Child's Play: An Activities and Materials Handbook.* Atlanta, GA: Humanics Learning, 1991.

Whordley, Derek, Ph.D and Rebecca J. Doster. *Humanics National Preschool Assessment Handbook.* Atlanta, GA: Humanics Learning, 1982.

ABOUT THE AUTHOR

For over ten years, Cynthia Manthey has taught preschool to children ages 2 to 5. She is a state Licensed Family Child Care Provider and currently acts as an Advisory Board Member for Project Team, "Together Everyone Accomplishes More," for her school district. Manthey also works as a part-time instructor in Early Childhood Education. She has had several articles on young children published and has conducted various workshops on topics such as self-esteem, positive discipline strategies, creative preschool curriculum, and multicultural preschool curriculum.

Manthey is also the author of *Pre-K Math: Concepts from Global Sources,* a companion book to this publication. Taking the same diverse, multicultural approach, *Pre-K Math* gives teachers and parents the resources and tools to introduce whole math concepts to children at a preschool level. In the past, Manthey's talents for innovative teaching and music composition led to *Music With Respect,* a children's musical cassette published by Quality Instructional Publications in 1992. This cassette, full of original songs and rhymes, was created to accompany her first book, *With Respect,* a valuable preschool teaching resource.